# The Challenges and Opportunities of Advance Care Planning

PROCEEDINGS OF A WORKSHOP

Laurene Graig, Kaitlyn Friedman, and Joe Alper, *Rapporteurs*

Roundtable on Quality Care for People with Serious Illness

Board on Health Care Services

Board on Health Sciences Policy

Health and Medicine Division

*The National Academies of*
SCIENCES · ENGINEERING · MEDICINE

THE NATIONAL ACADEMIES PRESS
Washington, DC
**www.nap.edu**

THE NATIONAL ACADEMIES PRESS   500 Fifth Street, NW   Washington, DC 20001

This activity was supported by Task Order No. 75N98F20P00009 with the National Institutes of Health's National Institute of Nursing Research and by the American Academy of Hospice and Palliative Medicine, American Geriatrics Society, Anthem, Ascension Health, Association of Professional Chaplains, Association of Rehabilitation Nurses, Blue Cross Blue Shield Association, Blue Cross Blue Shield of Arizona, Blue Cross Blue Shield of Massachusetts, Blue Cross Blue Shield of North Carolina, The California State University Shiley Institute for Palliative Care, Cambia Health Solutions, Cedars-Sinai Health System, Center to Advance Palliative Care, Centers for Medicare & Medicaid Services, Coalition to Transform Advanced Care, Excellus BlueCross BlueShield, Gordon and Betty Moore Foundation, The Greenwall Foundation, The John A. Hartford Foundation, Hospice & Palliative Nurses Association, Humana, Kaiser Permanente, National Academy for State Health Policy, National Coalition for Hospice and Palliative Care, National Hospice and Palliative Care Organization, National Palliative Care Research Center, National Patient Advocate Foundation, The New York Academy of Medicine, Patient-Centered Outcomes Research Institute, Social Work Hospice & Palliative Care Network, Supportive Care Coalition, University of Southern California Leonard D. Schaeffer Center for Health Policy & Economics, and the National Academy of Medicine.

International Standard Book Number-13: 978-0-309-44737-9
International Standard Book Number-10: 0-309-44737-2
Digital Object Identifier: https://doi.org/10.17226/26119

Additional copies of this publication are available from the National Academies Press, 500 Fifth Street, NW, Keck 360, Washington, DC 20001; (800) 624-6242 or (202) 334-3313; http://www.nap.edu.

Copyright 2021 by the National Academy of Sciences. All rights reserved.

Printed in the United States of America

Suggested citation: National Academies of Sciences, Engineering, and Medicine. 2021. *The challenges and opportunities of advance care planning: Proceedings of a workshop.* Washington, DC: The National Academies Press. https://doi.org/10.17226/26119.

# The National Academies of
## SCIENCES · ENGINEERING · MEDICINE

The **National Academy of Sciences** was established in 1863 by an Act of Congress, signed by President Lincoln, as a private, nongovernmental institution to advise the nation on issues related to science and technology. Members are elected by their peers for outstanding contributions to research. Dr. Marcia McNutt is president.

The **National Academy of Engineering** was established in 1964 under the charter of the National Academy of Sciences to bring the practices of engineering to advising the nation. Members are elected by their peers for extraordinary contributions to engineering. Dr. John L. Anderson is president.

The **National Academy of Medicine** (formerly the Institute of Medicine) was established in 1970 under the charter of the National Academy of Sciences to advise the nation on medical and health issues. Members are elected by their peers for distinguished contributions to medicine and health. Dr. Victor J. Dzau is president.

The three Academies work together as the **National Academies of Sciences, Engineering, and Medicine** to provide independent, objective analysis and advice to the nation and conduct other activities to solve complex problems and inform public policy decisions. The National Academies also encourage education and research, recognize outstanding contributions to knowledge, and increase public understanding in matters of science, engineering, and medicine.

Learn more about the National Academies of Sciences, Engineering, and Medicine at **www.nationalacademies.org**.

*The National Academies of*
SCIENCES · ENGINEERING · MEDICINE

**Consensus Study Reports** published by the National Academies of Sciences, Engineering, and Medicine document the evidence-based consensus on the study's statement of task by an authoring committee of experts. Reports typically include findings, conclusions, and recommendations based on information gathered by the committee and the committee's deliberations. Each report has been subjected to a rigorous and independent peer-review process and it represents the position of the National Academies on the statement of task.

**Proceedings** published by the National Academies of Sciences, Engineering, and Medicine chronicle the presentations and discussions at a workshop, symposium, or other event convened by the National Academies. The statements and opinions contained in proceedings are those of the participants and are not endorsed by other participants, the planning committee, or the National Academies.

For information about other products and activities of the National Academies, please visit www.nationalacademies.org/about/whatwedo.

## PLANNING COMMITTEE FOR A VIRTUAL WORKSHOP ON ADVANCE CARE PLANNING: CHALLENGES AND OPPORTUNITIES[1]

**ROBERT M. ARNOLD** (*Co-Chair*), Distinguished Service Professor of Medicine, University of Pittsburgh Medical Center
**JOANNE REIFSNYDER** (*Co-Chair*), Executive Vice President, Clinical Operations, and Chief Nursing Officer, Genesis HealthCare (*representing the Hospice and Palliative Care Nurses Association*)
**PATRICIA A. BOMBA,** Vice President and Medical Director, Geriatrics, Excellus BlueCross BlueShield; Chair, MOLST Statewide Implementation Team; Program Director, eMOLST; Chair, National Healthcare Decisions Day
**JANE CARMODY,** Program Officer, The John A. Hartford Foundation
**ANNA GOSLINE,** Senior Director of Strategic Initiatives, Blue Cross Blue Shield of Massachusetts; Executive Director, Massachusetts Coalition for Serious Illness Care
**DENISE HESS,** Director, Supportive Care Coalition, Catholic Health Association (*representing the Association of Professional Chaplains*)
**HAIDEN HUSKAMP,** 30th Anniversary Professor of Health Care Policy, Department of Health Care Policy, Harvard Medical School
**KIMBERLY SHERELL JOHNSON,** Associate Professor of Medicine, Senior Fellow in the Center for the Study of Aging and Human Development, Duke University School of Medicine
**REBECCA A. KIRCH,** Executive Vice President, Policy and Programs, National Patient Advocate Foundation
**BERNARD LO,** President Emeritus, The Greenwall Foundation
**R. SEAN MORRISON,** Co-Director, Patty and Jay Baker National Palliative Care Center; Director, National Palliative Care Research Center; Director, Hertzberg Palliative Care Institute; Hermann Merkin Professor of Palliative Care, Professor of Geriatrics and Palliative Medicine, Brookdale Department of Geriatrics and Palliative Medicine, Icahn School of Medicine at Mount Sinai

---

[1] The National Academies of Sciences, Engineering, and Medicine's planning committees are solely responsible for organizing the workshop, identifying topics, and choosing speakers. The responsibility for the published Proceedings of a Workshop rests with the workshop rapporteurs and the institution.

**JUDITH R. PERES,** Board Member, Social Work Hospice and Palliative Care Network
**LEONARD D. SCHAEFFER,** Judge Robert Maclay Widney Chair and Professor, University of Southern California
**REBECCA SUDORE,** Professor of Medicine, University of California, San Francisco, School of Medicine
**JAMES A. TULSKY,** Chair, Department of Psychosocial Oncology and Palliative Care, Dana-Farber Cancer Institute; Chief, Division of Palliative Medicine, Department of Medicine, Brigham and Women's Hospital; Co-Director, Harvard Medical School Center for Palliative Care; Professor of Medicine, Harvard Medical School

*Project Staff*

**LAURENE GRAIG,** Director, Roundtable on Quality Care for People with Serious Illness
**KAITLYN FRIEDMAN,** Associate Program Officer
**ANESIA WILKS,** Senior Program Assistant
**SHARYL NASS,** Senior Director, Board on Health Care Services, and Director, National Cancer Policy Forum

*Consultant*

**JOE ALPER,** Consulting Writer

# ROUNDTABLE ON QUALITY CARE FOR PEOPLE WITH SERIOUS ILLNESS[1]

**PEGGY MAGUIRE** (*Co-Chair*), President and Board Chair, Cambia Health Foundation

**JAMES A. TULSKY** (*Co-Chair*), Chair, Department of Psychosocial Oncology and Palliative Care, Dana-Farber Cancer Institute; Chief, Division of Palliative Medicine, Department of Medicine, Brigham and Women's Hospital; Co-Director, Harvard Medical School Center for Palliative Care; Professor of Medicine, Harvard Medical School

**KIRK ALLEN,** Senior Vice President, Home Care, Humana

**JENNIFER BALLENTINE,** Executive Director, The California State University Shiley Institute for Palliative Care

**ROBERT A. BERGAMINI,** SSM Health (*representing the Supportive Care Coalition*)

**LORI BISHOP,** Vice President of Palliative and Advanced Care, National Hospice and Palliative Care Organization

**PATRICIA A. BOMBA,** Vice President and Medical Director, Geriatrics, Excellus BlueCross BlueShield; Chair, MOLST Statewide Implementation Team; Program Director, eMOLST; Chair, National Healthcare Decisions Day

**KAREN BULLOCK,** Professor, John A. Hartford Faculty Scholar, Department of Social Work, North Carolina State University (*representing the Social Work Hospice and Palliative Care Network*)

**GRACE B. CAMPBELL,** Assistant Professor, Department of Acute and Tertiary Care, University of Pittsburgh School of Nursing (*representing the Association of Rehabilitation Nurses*)

**JOHN CAMPBELL,** Senior Medical Director, Clinical Effectiveness, Blue Cross Blue Shield of North Carolina

**JANE CARMODY,** Program Officer, The John A. Hartford Foundation

**STEVE CLAUSER,** Director, Healthcare Delivery and Disparities Research Program, Patient-Centered Outcomes Research Institute

**SARAH DAMIANO,** Director, Palliative Care, Clinical and Network Services, Ascension Health

---

[1] The National Academies of Sciences, Engineering, and Medicine's forums and roundtables do not issue, review, or approve individual documents. The responsibility for the published Proceedings of a Workshop rests with the workshop rapporteurs and the institution.

**DAVID J. DEBONO,** National Medical Directory for Oncology, Anthem
**CAROLE REDDING FLAMM,** Executive Medical Director, Center for Clinical Value, Office of Clinical Affairs, Blue Cross Blue Shield Association
**ANNA GOSLINE,** Senior Director of Strategic Initiatives, Blue Cross Blue Shield of Massachusetts; Executive Director, Massachusetts Coalition for Serious Illness Care
**MICHELLE GROMAN,** President and Chief Executive Officer, The Greenwell Foundation
**DENISE HESS,** Director, Supportive Care Coalition, Catholic Health Association (*representing the Association of Professional Chaplains*)
**PAMELA S. HINDS,** Director and Professor, Conway Chair in Nursing Research; Director Nursing Research and Quality Outcomes, Children's National Health System
**HAIDEN HUSKAMP,** 30th Anniversary Professor of Health Care Policy, Department of Health Care Policy, Harvard Medical School
**KIMBERLY SHERELL JOHNSON,** Associate Professor of Medicine, Senior Fellow in the Center for the Study of Aging and Human Development, Duke University School of Medicine
**REBECCA A. KIRCH,** Executive Vice President, Policy and Programs, National Patient Advocate Foundation
**TOM KOUTSOUMPAS,** Co-Founder, Coalition to Transform Advanced Care; President and Chief Executive Officer, National Partnership for Hospice Innovation
**SHARI M. LING,** Deputy Chief Medical Officer, Center for Clinical Standards and Quality, Centers for Medicare & Medicaid Services
**DIANE E. MEIER,** Director, Center to Advance Palliative Care; Gaisman Professor of Medical Ethics, Vice Chair for Public Policy and Professor, Department of Geriatrics and Palliative Medicine, Department of Medicine, Icahn School of Medicine at Mount Sinai
**AMY MELNICK,** Executive Director, National Coalition for Hospice and Palliative Care
**JERI L. MILLER,** Chief, Office of End-of-Life and Palliative Care Research, Senior Policy Analysis, Division of Extramural Science Programs, National Institute of Nursing Research, National Institutes of Health

**R. SEAN MORRISON,** Co-Director, Patty and Jay Baker National Palliative Care Center; Director, National Palliative Care Research Center; Director, Hertzberg Palliative Care Institute; Hermann Merkin Professor of Palliative Care, Professor of Geriatrics and Palliative Medicine, Brookdale Department of Geriatrics and Palliative Medicine, Icahn School of Medicine at Mount Sinai

**PHILIP A. PIZZO,** Founding Director, Stanford Distinguished Careers Institute; Former Dean and David and Susan Heckerman Professor of Pediatrics and of Microbiology and Immunology, Stanford School of Medicine

**THOMAS M. PRISELAC,** President and Chief Executive Officer, Cedars-Sinai Health System

**KITTY PURINGTON,** Senior Program Director, National Academy for State Health Policy

**RUBINA RAJA,** Medical Director, Operations, Blue Cross Blue Shield of Arizona

**JOANNE REIFSNYDER,** Executive Vice President, Clinical Operations, and Chief Nursing Officer, Genesis HealthCare (*representing the Hospice and Palliative Nurses Association*)

**PHILLIP RODGERS,** Professor, Family Medicine and Internal Medicine; Director, Adult Palliative Medicine Clinical Programs, University of Michigan (*representing the American Academy of Hospice and Palliative Medicine*)

**JUDITH A. SALERNO,** President, The New York Academy of Medicine

**LEONARD D. SCHAEFFER,** Judge Robert Maclay Widney Chair and Professor, University of Southern California

**JOSEPH W. SHEGA,** Senior Vice President and Chief Medical Officer, VITAS Hospice Care (*representing the American Geriatrics Society*)

**SUSAN ELIZABETH WANG,** WLA Chief, Department of Geriatrics, Palliative, and Continuing Care; Fellowship Director, Palliative Medicine; Regional Lead, Shared Decision-Making and Advance Care Planning, Southern California Permanente Medical Group, Kaiser Permanente

*Roundtable on Quality Care for People with Serious Illness Staff*

**LAURENE GRAIG,** Director, Roundtable on Quality Care for People with Serious Illness

**KAITLYN FRIEDMAN,** Associate Program Officer

**ANESIA WILKS**, Senior Program Assistant
**MICAH WINOGRAD,** Senior Finance Business Partner
**SHARYL NASS,** Senior Director, Board on Health Care Services, and Director, National Cancer Policy Forum
**ANDREW M. POPE,** Senior Director, Board on Health Sciences Policy

# Reviewers

This Proceedings of a Workshop was reviewed in draft form by individuals chosen for their diverse perspectives and technical expertise. The purpose of this independent review is to provide candid and critical comments that will assist the National Academies of Sciences, Engineering, and Medicine in making each published proceedings as sound as possible and to ensure that it meets the institutional standards for quality, objectivity, evidence, and responsiveness to the charge. The review comments and draft manuscript remain confidential to protect the integrity of the process.

We thank the following individuals for their review of this proceedings:

**RANDALL CURTIS,** Cambia Palliative Care Center of Excellence, University of Washington
**SUSAN HICKMAN,** Regenstreif Institute, Indiana University Schools of Nursing and Medicine, IUPUI RESPECT Signature Center
**MILDRED Z. SOLOMON,** The Hastings Center

Although the reviewers listed above provided many constructive comments and suggestions, they were not asked to endorse the content of the proceedings nor did they see the final draft before its release. The review of this proceedings was overseen by **KATHLEEN UNROE,** Indiana University Center for Aging and Indiana University School of Medicine. She was responsible for making certain that an independent examination of this proceedings was carried out in accordance with standards of the National Academies and that all review comments were carefully considered. Responsibility for the final content rests entirely with the rapporteurs and the National Academies.

# Acknowledgments

The National Academies of Sciences, Engineering, and Medicine's Roundtable on Quality Care for People with Serious Illness wishes to express its sincere gratitude to the planning committee co-chairs Robert Arnold and JoAnne Reifsnyder for their valuable contributions to the development and orchestration of this workshop. The roundtable also wishes to thank all the members of the planning committee, who collaborated to ensure a workshop replete with informative presentations and rich discussions. Finally, the roundtable wants to thank the speakers and moderators, who generously shared their expertise and their time with workshop participants.

Support from the many annual sponsors of the Roundtable on Quality Care for People with Serious Illness is critical to its work. The sponsors include the National Institutes of Health's National Institute of Nursing Research and the American Academy of Hospice and Palliative Medicine, American Geriatrics Society, Anthem, Ascension Health, Association of Professional Chaplains, Association of Rehabilitation Nurses, Blue Cross Blue Shield Association, Blue Cross Blue Shield of Arizona, Blue Cross Blue Shield of Massachusetts, Blue Cross Blue Shield of North Carolina, The California State University Shiley Institute for Palliative Care, Cambia Health Solutions, Cedars-Sinai Health System, Center to Advance Palliative Care, Centers for Medicare & Medicaid Services, Coalition to Transform Advanced Care, Excellus BlueCross BlueShield, Gordon and Betty Moore Foundation, The Greenwall Foundation, The John A. Hartford Foundation, Hospice

& Palliative Nurses Association, Humana, Kaiser Permanente, National Academy for State Health Policy, National Coalition for Hospice and Palliative Care, National Hospice and Palliative Care Organization, National Palliative Care Research Center, National Patient Advocate Foundation, The New York Academy of Medicine, Patient-Centered Outcomes Research Institute, Social Work Hospice & Palliative Care Network, Supportive Care Coalition, University of Southern California Leonard D. Schaeffer Center for Health Policy & Economics, and the National Academy of Medicine.

# Contents

| | |
|---|---|
| ACRONYMS AND ABBREVIATIONS | xix |
| PROCEEDINGS OF A WORKSHOP | 1 |
| INTRODUCTION | 1 |
| OPENING REMARKS | 2 |
| THE PARADOX OF ADVANCE CARE PLANNING | 7 |

    Lived Experiences with Advance Care Planning, 7
    An Ethical Framework: From Advance Directives to Advance Care Planning, 9
    The Complexities of Advance Care Planning: What Are We Even Talking About?, 11
    Discussion, 16

| | |
|---|---|
| INTERPRETING THE EVIDENCE BASE FOR ADVANCE CARE PLANNING | 17 |

    What Is the Evidence and Why Does It Matter?, 17
    How Clinical and Health Care Leaders Use Advance Care Planning Research, 21
    Making Sense of the Evidence, 24
    Advance Care Planning Is a Right: A Medical–Legal Perspective, 28
    Discussion, 31

| | |
|---|---|
| A BRIEF SUMMARY OF THE FIRST WEBINAR | 35 |

**THINKING DIFFERENTLY ABOUT ADVANCE CARE PLANNING**    37
    Flaws in Advance Care Planning Implementation and
        Evaluation, 37
    Advance Care Planning: Ethical Challenges, 41
    Advancing the Language of Advance Care Planning:
        A Messaging Research Project, 43
    Discussion, 46
**PRACTICAL STEPS TO MORE EFFECTIVE ADVANCE CARE PLANNING**    48
    The Importance of Patients' and Families' Nonmedical
        Concerns, 48
    Implementing Advance Care Planning in the Hospital
        Setting, 50
    The Health System Perspective on Practical Steps to More
        Effective Advance Care Planning, 51
    Discussion, 54
**PANEL DISCUSSION**    57
**CLOSING REMARKS**    62
**REFERENCES**    62

**APPENDIX A**: Statement of Task    69
**APPENDIX B**: Workshop Agenda    71

# Box, Figures, and Table

## BOX

1   Suggestions Made by Individual Workshop Participants to Address the Challenges and Opportunities for Advance Care Planning (ACP), 3

## FIGURES

1   A model showing how the conversations about advance care planning and documentation may differ from decisions about goals of care or consent for treatment, 13
2   The continuum of communication and decision making in serious illness care, 26
3   Advanced serious illness preparation and planning, 28
4   Seriously ill, hospitalized patients rated whether various states of functional disability were better or worse than death, 39

## TABLE

1   Five Messages Supporting Advance Care Planning, 45

# Acronyms and Abbreviations

| | |
|---|---|
| ACP | advance care planning |
| CCCC | Community Conversations on Compassionate Care |
| CPR | cardiopulmonary resuscitation |
| ED | emergency department |
| EHR | electronic health record |
| ICU | intensive care unit |
| MOLST | medical orders for life-sustaining treatment |
| NPAF | National Patient Advocate Foundation |
| POLST | physician orders for life-sustaining treatment |
| PTSD | posttraumatic stress disorder |
| RCT | randomized controlled trial |

# Proceedings of a Workshop

## INTRODUCTION[1]

Advance care planning (ACP) has long been a staple of caring for people with serious illness. Over its long history, it has been defined in different ways. A recent Delphi[2] panel offered a consensus definition of ACP as "[a] process that supports adults at any age or stage of health in understanding and sharing their personal values, life goals, and preferences regarding future medical care" (Sudore et al., 2017). Even this definition, however, was written with the expectation that it would evolve over time to fully capture the complexity of ACP.

ACP is designed to prepare people for unexpected events, be it a medical emergency or an acute, chronic, or terminal illness. The hope is that ACP can contribute to improved quality of life by relieving unnecessary suffering, and by clarifying the complex and often complicated decisions that need to be made by the individual and their caregivers. ACP also aims to ease

---

[1] The planning committee's role was limited to planning the workshop, and the Proceedings of a Workshop was prepared by the workshop rapporteurs as a factual summary of what occurred at the workshop. Statements, recommendations, and opinions expressed are those of individual presenters and participants, and are not necessarily endorsed or verified by the National Academies of Sciences, Engineering, and Medicine, and they should not be construed as reflecting any group consensus.

[2] The Delphi method is a process used to arrive at a group opinion or decision by surveying a panel of experts.

the burden of decision making on the part of family members should the individual become unable to make decisions for themself (Sudore and Fried, 2010), as well as lessen moral distress among health care providers (Elpern et al., 2005; Ulrich and Grady, 2019).

Clinicians, researchers, patients, and the public have developed a variety of perspectives about the many aspects of ACP, ranging from the definition to the timing, goals, outcomes, and value of ACP. Moreover, despite significant efforts over the past three decades to raise visibility and promote completing an advance directive,[3] one component of ACP, less than 40 percent of Americans—including adults with chronic illnesses—have done so (Rao et al., 2014; Yadav et al., 2017).

To better understand the challenges and opportunities for ACP, acknowledge and highlight divergent viewpoints, and examine what is empirically known and not known about ACP and its outcomes, the National Academies of Sciences, Engineering, and Medicine's Roundtable on Quality Care for People with Serious Illness hosted a virtual public workshop, Advance Care Planning: Challenges and Opportunities, on October 26 and November 2, 2020. The workshop explored the paradox of ACP, its evidence base, ways to think differently about ACP, and various approaches to making it more effective.

This Proceedings of a Workshop summarizes the presentations and discussions from that workshop. The speakers, panelists, and workshop participants presented a broad range of views and ideas, and Box 1 provides a summary of individual participants' suggestions for potential actions. Appendixes A and B contain the workshop's Statement of Task and agenda, respectively. The speakers' presentations have been archived online (as PDF and video files).[4]

## OPENING REMARKS

James Tulsky from the Dana-Farber Cancer Institute, Brigham and Women's Hospital, and Harvard Medical School opened the workshop, explaining that roundtable members had wondered whether there was

---

[3] An advance directive is a written statement of a person's wishes regarding medical treatment, often including a living will, which is made to ensure those wishes are carried out should the person be unable to communicate them.

[4] For more information, see https://www.nationalacademies.org/our-work/advance-care-planning-challenges-and-opportunities-a-workshop (accessed December 9, 2020).

> **BOX 1**
> **Suggestions Made by Individual Workshop Participants to Address the Challenges and Opportunities for Advance Care Planning (ACP)**
>
> **Communicating About ACP to Enhance Understanding of Its Role and Importance**
> - Involve patients and caregivers in defining what ACP means to those outside the health care field. (Sudore)
> - Use patient advocates to relay personal stories that can serve as a powerful spark to start the necessary dialogue that people need to have with their loved ones. (Stuart)
> - Provide follow-up care from a case manager or clergy member to help individuals and family members process that the end of life is near. (Stuart)
> - Shift from the current language framed around making treatment decisions in advance for end-of-life care to an approach that tries to provide optimal, person-centered medical care for people with serious illness and uncertainty if they are experiencing the end of life. (Heyland)
> - Continue working toward culture change that integrates ACP and health care planning in the same way that legal planning and financial planning have already been well integrated into everyday life. (Bomba)
> - Promote a better understanding of the potential future of those with serious illness. (Dresser)
> - Develop a multi-tiered marketing strategy that contains a layered, congruent effort that occurs in health systems, communities, and on a national basis and that includes language and messaging that speak to the masses. (Perrilliat)
>
> **Preparing Clinicians to Have High-Quality ACP Conversations**
> - Focus on becoming more trustworthy and preparing individuals and their trusted loved ones to engage in health care decision making. (Montgomery)
> - Scan ACP documents and have them on a phone so they are handy whenever needed. (Harris)
> - Embrace the shift in power at the point of decision making and have clinicians accept that they cannot know the right care to deliver without knowing what matters most to the person for whom they are caring. (Montgomery)
>
> *continued*

## BOX 1 Continued

- Do not skip the important step of preparing the patient with discussions about their illness; their prognosis; their fears, goals, and values; and the trade-offs that come with any decision. (Heyland)
- Use more sophisticated decision aids to elicit authentic value statements and support decision making throughout the course of serious illness. (Heyland)
- Cover different content when doing early ACP versus when the end of life is more proximal. (Montgomery)
- Focus on deliberation and discussion between the individual and their surrogates rather than solely aiming to complete specific directives or written documents. (Lo, Sudore)
- Incentivize training as an accountability measure to reinforce the importance of having ACP conversations. (Kirch)
- Participate in the VitalTalk program as a clinician before seeing patients. (Kirch)
- Make it easy to find ACP documentation in a patient's electronic health record, document the values and reasons behind decision making in discussions about goals of care, and carry previous decisions forward intelligently. (Childers)
- Fulfill the ethical obligation of ensuring high-quality ACP conversations, a conversation that is a safe experience for patients, and consistency across the health system in what patients and families experience. (O'Connor)
- Use conversation anchors or guides to help keep clinicians' comments open-ended. (Childers)
- Have trainees do a palliative care rotation early in their career to normalize ACP as a part of medical care. (Childers)
- Use platforms such as electronic medical orders for life-sustaining treatment to improve quality through standardized conversation elements, increased accessibility, and real-time updating. (Bomba)

**Using a Person-Centered, Holistic Approach to ACP**
- Take a broader, more holistic approach for ACP programs, use rigorous implementation science research principles, and consider multiple stakeholders, context, culture, and workflows. (Sudore)
- Develop approaches to ACP that recognize the interests and concerns of people with dementia and other intellectual disabilities. (Dresser)

- Recognize how stigma can shape individual preferences, professional judgments, and community attitudes. (Dresser)
- Value and support caregiving as a major cost-sharing and quality care delivery contribution. (Kirch)
- Listen to an individual's life priorities and preferences when talking about treatment benefits, costs, and trade-offs. (Gosline)
- Examine ACP from a holistic perspective that operates both within and outside the medical system to involve the community beyond the health care system. (Perrilliat)
- Stop traumatizing caregivers and the people they care for in the complex decision-making process by reframing decisions around who the individual is and their wishes rather than specific dichotomous medical decisions. (Brody)

**Measuring and Evaluating ACP**
- Define outcomes for each stakeholder (patient, surrogate, clinician, health system) and clinical context. (Sudore)
- Foster culture change, build patient-centered systems, and establish metrics that are different for the general population versus those facing end of life. (Bomba)
- Include pragmatic trials as part of future ACP research so as to better measure and evaluate the challenges of an evolving complex process across various stakeholders and in real-life situations. (Montgomery)
- Address the heterogeneity of ACP by working at a higher level of granularity, which will allow greater specification of what does and does not work. (Heyland)
- Design new ways to help people articulate their goals and strategies to measure concordance with these goals. (Halpern)
- Measure whether people feel they are in control, listened to, and supported in their decision making. (Gosline)
- Scale training to ensure consistent, high-quality ACP conversations, use data science to identify patients to prioritize, define the target population (e.g., patients with serious illness and frailty), and track and monitor conversations for ongoing program evaluation. (O'Connor)

**Changing the Focus of ACP**
- Focus ACP efforts for patients and surrogates on preparing them with the skills needed to make in-the-moment decisions and communicate with each other and the clinical team. (Sudore)

*continued*

> **BOX 1 Continued**
>
> - Narrow the focus of ACP to appointing a health care proxy and preparing people to have productive conversations about end-of-life care and what their primary needs and concerns are. (Gosline, Kirch, Morrison, O'Connor)
> - Focus on better preparing patients and surrogates to make decisions in the moment rather than using a document that has limited validity and clinical utility to make such decisions in advance. (Heyland)
> - Prepare people for in-the-moment clinical decisions, recognizing that having laypeople, even seriously ill people, make hypothetical decisions that are expected to be followed in the future risks medical error. (Heyland, Morrison)
> - Expand thoughts about what ACP means and what it can be beyond the health care system to address community-based needs and take advantage of the resources that are available to support those pressing needs. (Kirch)
> - Stop conflating ACP with cost savings and reduced health care use. (Meier)
> - Stop worshiping autonomy and the focus on individualism, and instead concentrate on beneficence, care and justice, and accountability of the clinical staff to initiate conversations and speak frankly. (Solomon)

anything new to say about ACP given that it is one of the most thoroughly researched areas in serious illness care. "As we were discussing this," said Tulsky, "what became very clear was that this was in fact an area of intense controversy, where there were many different opinions about the value of ACP, in what situations ACP would be most effective, what the definition should be, and the key questions that needed to get answered."

Tulsky also noted that the controversy related to ACP has been amplified by the COVID-19 pandemic. "So many of us have unfortunately seen patients who have had to make decisions about life-sustaining treatments, oftentimes with little advance notice, and this has heightened concern about the need for advance care planning," he said.

In his opening comments, Robert Arnold from the University of Pittsburgh Medical Center predicted that vigorous differences of opinion would come to light during the course of the two webinars. While the

**Improving ACP Through Policy- and Systems-Level Change**
- Establish a reimbursement system for ACP that incentivizes value-based care so that there is residential monitoring and a backup plan for people, instead of rushing them to the hospital in an emergency. (Halpern)
- Prepare people for serious illness decisions by promoting a life-long experience with and expectation of shared decision making with trusted health care clinicians in health care systems that are focused on cultural humility, respect, aligning care with priorities, and identifying and addressing bias and structural racism. (Gosline)
- Formalize accountability within quality and payment systems for person-centered communication skills, training, and practice that identifies patients' priorities and meets their needs. (Kirch)
- Build a scalable workforce for ACP that does not rely solely on palliative care specialists. (O'Connor)
- Reallocate funds to embrace the idea that ACP is an important human-centric initiative that is going to impact everyone, regardless of whether they are in health care. (Perrilliat)
- Include and engage with policy makers to develop policy that addresses justice, equity, and inclusion. (Perrilliat)

notion of patient-centered care is something that all of the webinar participants care about and spend their time working toward, Arnold said, the question is whether and how ACP helps us or distracts us from achieving that goal. Throughout this workshop, "you will get a sense of where the disagreement lies and be able to come to your own conclusions about what the next steps should be," concluded Arnold.

## THE PARADOX OF ADVANCE CARE PLANNING

### Lived Experiences with Advance Care Planning

The first session of the workshop opened with Maureen Stuart and Wyvonia Woods Harris, both volunteers with the National Patient Advocate Foundation (NPAF), sharing their lived experiences of caring for someone with serious illness. They spoke of the complexity of communicating with and about a family member's preferences and values, and ensuring that a loved one's wishes are followed at the end of life. Speaking first, Stuart recounted her father's last days fighting advanced prostate cancer. When diagnosed, her father was adamant that he did not want to die in a hospital. However, her father did not want to discuss his other preferences or wishes for end-of-life care with any of his children, nor did he want to complete an advance directive. Stuart explained that her father's oncologist tried to communicate with his primary care doctor about preferences for end-of-life care, but it became clear that the choices were to go to a hospital or rely on the family to provide care, because palliative care and hospice services were not accessible where he lived in rural northern California. As her father's cancer steadily advanced, his oncologist informed him of the Death with Dignity Act[5] and encouraged him to decide if he wanted to start the process before he became cognitively impaired. Stuart's father told her, but not his other daughter or his son, that he wanted to take advantage of that option, which was available to him because his oncology care took place in Oregon. Stuart pointed out that it was only then that her father acknowledged that his cancer was terminal.

Stuart explained that her father asked her to keep his decision a secret because he believed that the rest of the family would not support his decision. Stuart said her father did not express or document any other desires, except to die in his own bed at home and to have his family present, which left decisions about infection control, hydration, and other clinical choices to her. His death was quick and painful, and it did not allow for a lot of time for conversations about his goals of care. "I thought I knew what he probably wanted," said Stuart, but she added that the gap he left regarding his specific wishes left her second-guessing her choices even 4 years after his death.

When asked what might have helped her during that time, Stuart said that while his oncology team provided wonderful care, there was no follow-up by a case manager or clergy member after the family was told that there was "probably nothing else" that the clinical care team could do for their father. As a result, the family was left to its own devices. "I think if we had been bolstered or had access to some mental health providers or a case manager, that probably would have helped tremendously," said Stuart.

---

[5] For more information, see https://www.deathwithdignity.org (accessed December 9, 2020).

Harris then spoke about her husband's journey with chronic illness, which began when he was diagnosed with hypertension at age 34. At age 40, he developed Crohn's disease, for which he had several surgeries. He then had kidney problems, developed polymyositis (an inflammatory disease that causes muscle weakness affecting both sides of the body), and needed his gallbladder removed. In 2017, while hospitalized as a result of complications from kidney disease, he developed pulmonary edema[6] and suffered a heart attack. Over the next 2 years, he was on dialysis and had both legs amputated.

When Harris and her family had started preparing advance directives, her husband had indicated that he did not want any "heroic measures." However, those plans were interrupted when her husband needed surgery to repair an intestinal blockage and he expressed a desire to live despite his precarious medical condition. Harris described how although her husband's primary care physician was aware of his wishes as expressed in his advance directive, that knowledge was lost when a hospitalist took over his care. The lack of a written plan at the hospital proved to be a significant issue at a subsequent time when her husband needed emergency surgery late at night and the surgeon, from another hospital, knew nothing about him and his treatment preferences. She further described how her husband's preferences had changed again, and she had to tell the new clinicians not to intubate him when he coded following the emergency surgery. Harris emphasized that emergency departments (EDs) and intensive care units (ICUs) are not good places to start the ACP process. Reflecting back on that experience, Harris suggested that everyone not only have an advance care plan, but also scan it into their phones so as to have it readily available whenever needed.

## An Ethical Framework: From Advance Directives to Advance Care Planning

Bernard Lo, president emeritus of The Greenwall Foundation, began by describing how on a winter day in 1983, Nancy Cruzan skidded off a Missouri highway, and suffered a serious brain injury when her car crashed. Though resuscitated, Cruzan never regained consciousness and was in a persistent vegetative state. After 3 years, her parents realized there was no hope that she would regain consciousness, and they asked to have her feed-

---

[6] Pulmonary edema is a condition caused by excess fluid in the lungs.

ing tube removed. Lo explained that the U.S. Supreme Court ruled that Missouri could only do so if she had executed a signed, legal document or made an oral statement rejecting that specific intervention in that situation. The Court ruled, for example, that the oral statements Cruzan had made to her parents indicating that she "did not want to live as a vegetable" were not sufficient (U.S. Supreme Court, 1990).

Lo explained that the ruling led to a national focus on advance directives, and many states passed laws authorizing an individual to appoint a health care proxy. In 1990, Congress passed the Patient Self-Determination Act,[7] which required hospitals, skilled nursing facilities, home health agencies, hospice programs, and health maintenance organizations to (1) inform patients of their rights under state law to make decisions concerning their medical care; (2) periodically inquire as to whether a patient has executed an advance directive and document the patient's wishes regarding their medical care; (3) not discriminate against persons who have executed an advance directive; (4) ensure that legally valid advance directives and documented medical care wishes are implemented to the extent permitted by state law; and (5) provide educational programs for staff, patients, and the community on ethical issues concerning patient self-determination and advance directives. At the time, this case triggered the idea that everyone, even young, healthy individuals, should complete an advance directive, though Lo noted that this thinking may have changed in the subsequent years.

Written advance directives or specific oral statements have their limitations, said Lo, particularly because no one can anticipate the actual clinical situations and decisions that will arise. For example, he had a patient who said she never wanted to go to the hospital, but when she broke her hip and was in terrible pain, she had to reconsider that wish if she wanted her pain adequately relieved. In addition, an individual may realize that these decisions are complicated and want to give the family leeway to consider not what the individual would have wanted, but rather what the best decision is in the current situation, said Lo.

Lo noted that the focus on specific directives and written documents overlooks what may be more important: deliberation and discussion between the individual and their surrogates, whether that is the family, the physician, or both. In fact, he said, ACP is less about the document or one specific directive and more about the process of discussions. That process, he

---

[7] Additional information is available at https://www.congress.gov/bill/101st-congress/house-bill/4449 (accessed December 9, 2020).

added, starts not with specific medical interventions but rather with understanding an individual's core values. In Lo's view, ACP should be about not only withholding interventions but also preferences regarding a good death. Lo added, as Stuart noted earlier, that one of the hopes of ACP is that it relieves the burdens on surrogates who are making decisions in situations that are typically complicated and unanticipated.

Lo explained that the question that often arises and is hard to articulate in ACP is how much pain and suffering the individual is willing to endure, for how long, and for what benefit. One decision a person can make concerns the transition to palliative care. Many of Lo's patients have said they want some reasonable attempts made to treat reversible problems, but only up to a point. However, defining that point in advance is difficult, Lo pointed out. He also noted that the Cruzan case is one example of the shift toward experts saying that it is appropriate in some cases to base decisions on the patient's values, goals of care, and current best interests as interpreted by the appropriate surrogate. Over time, "this country legally, ethically, and religiously has made a huge shift to where we are now trusting the discretion and judgment of surrogates, who are often close family members," said Lo.

In closing, Lo underscored that ACP does not and could not resolve all problems with end-of-life care. Even when ACP goes well, said Lo, decisions are difficult, and unanticipated decisions will still need to be made.

## The Complexities of Advance Care Planning: What Are We Even Talking About?

Rebecca Sudore, professor at the University of California, San Francisco, School of Medicine, began her remarks by explaining that the original definition of ACP focused on making treatment decisions in advance, such as deciding about resuscitation or mechanical ventilation. This definition, however, did not account for issues related to the difficulty of predicting future contexts, the ability of humans to adapt to new circumstances and change their minds, and extrapolating treatment decisions about resuscitation to other decisions. As Sudore explained, the most important reason to reconsider this original definition is research showing that what matters most to individuals is not the treatment but rather its outcome and what life will be like afterward (Fried et al., 2002, 2006; Gillick, 2004; Halpern and Arnold, 2008; Lockhart et al., 2001; Loewenstein, 2005; McMahan et al., 2013; Pearlman et al., 2005; Perkins, 2007; Quill, 2000; Ubel, 2005; Ubel et al., 2005; Winter et al., 2003).

Sudore and her colleagues convened a large, international Delphi panel to develop a new definition of ACP, which states that it is a "process that supports adults at any age or stage of health in understanding and sharing their personal values, life goals, and preferences regarding future medical care" (Sudore et al., 2017). Sudore explained that even as she and her colleagues were writing the paper proposing this revised definition, they stated that it was a starting point that would need to be revisited as the field matured. "I think we are learning that ACP is much more complex than this," she explained. She noted that ACP has had many meanings and definitions and that when studies are being done or recommendations are being made, it is important to first describe the definition that is being used in that context.

Sudore referenced an organizational framework from Respecting Choices,[8] an evidence-based model of ACP, which outlines "first steps," "next steps," and "advanced steps." Sudore said these steps can apply to the trajectory of someone's life course and their readiness to engage in the ACP process. For example, people in advanced stages of their life course may still be at the first steps of readiness to engage in ACP.

Sudore explained that ACP that focuses on values, wishes, and preferences involves a different kind of conversation than one that focuses on goals of care, in-the-moment decision making, or consent for a specific treatment (Sinuff et al., 2015) (see Figure 1). These conversations may differ based on the setting, such as the home versus the hospital, but each category (ACP, documentation, decisions about goals of care, or consent for treatment) has distinct components that guide conversations with patients. Sudore noted that the majority of the conversations she has with individuals, both as a geriatrics primary care physician and as an inpatient palliative care physician, involve values, wishes, and preferences, as listed under the Advance Care Planning section of Figure 1, rather than conversations about consent for a specific treatment.

Sudore further explained that ACP is influenced by the complex interplay of many stakeholders, including patients, surrogates, the community where social norms are established, clinicians, the health system and its ability to electronically retrieve ACP information, and the laws and policy that support ACP (McMahan et al., 2020). Sudore noted that in addition to this complexity, one of the major challenges for ACP is that that no single professional group or service line "owns" or is responsible for ACP.

---

[8] Additional information is available at https://respectingchoices.org (accessed December 9, 2020).

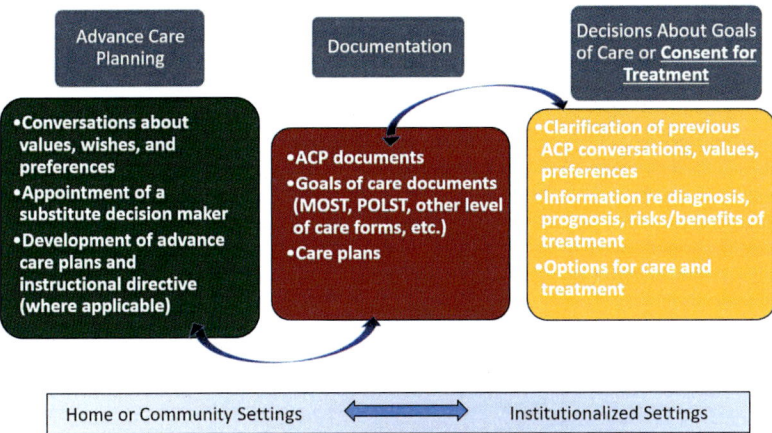

**FIGURE 1** A model showing how the conversations about advance care planning and documentation may differ from decisions about goals of care or consent for treatment.
NOTE: ACP = advance care planning; MOLST = medical orders for life-sustaining treatment; POLST = physician orders for life-sustaining treatment.
SOURCES: Rebecca Sudore presentation, October 26, 2020; adapted from Sinuff et al., 2015.

Additional complex factors are involved as well, including the existing injustices and health disparities that the COVID-19 pandemic has exacerbated. "Millions of Americans do not have access to clinicians, health systems, or [insurance] policies that would support access to trained clinicians who could walk people step-by-step through the ACP process," said Sudore, "and given the large amount of justified mistrust, some communities will only do ACP outside the clinical setting with their families and friends."

Given this complexity, Sudore further explained, it may not be reasonable to expect an ACP intervention targeted to one or a few of these stakeholders to be able to positively affect all outcomes and solve all of the problems of the nation's broken health care system. ACP definitions and reasonable outcomes may need to be defined for each stakeholder and setting.

Sudore pointed out that the interplay between these many complex factors has raised the question of why anyone should even attempt ACP, and she answered that the most important reason not to abandon ACP is that patients, surrogates, and clinicians express the need and desire for it, particularly if they have had experiences making serious medical decisions for themselves or others (McMahan et al., 2020). Clinicians cannot make recommendations or guide care decisions without knowing a patient's values and needs, which, in Sudore's view, requires that patients and surrogates be prepared to communicate that information (Perkins, 2007; Torke et al., 2009). "Without some form of preparation, patients and surrogates will not be able to communicate their values effectively, and this is especially true when people are under stress and when they have no prior relationship with the clinicians they may find themselves interacting with in a crisis situation," explained Sudore. In an effort to help prepare individuals and their surrogate decision makers, Sudore and her colleagues developed the person-centered Prepare for Your Care program[9] (Sudore and Fried, 2010; Sudore et al., 2018b). Similar programs include Advance Care Planning Decisions,[10] the Plan Well Guide,[11] and community-based tools, such as those offered by the Conversation Project.[12]

Sudore explained that research shows that patients want to talk to their clinicians about ACP, they expect health care providers to initiate ACP conversations, and they view it as a way to prepare surrogates and decrease their decisional burden. In her view, clinicians value ACP as an important part of their jobs to help prepare patients and families for making decisions. However, she noted, research has produced mixed results related to measuring outcomes (Bischoff et al., 2013; Bond et al., 2018; Detering et al., 2010; Houben et al., 2014; Jimenez et al., 2018; Silveira et al., 2010; Sudore et al., 2018a). In some studies, ACP is associated with increased advance directive completion, increased patient satisfaction with care, improved quality-of-life and goal-concordant care, increased surrogate–clinician communication, and decreased stress for the surrogate decision maker. However, a 2018 review of 80 systematic reviews revealed that many ACP studies, as well as the systematic reviews themselves, were deemed to be of low quality. Sudore noted that the low-quality research makes it difficult to develop definitive recommendations (Jimenez et al., 2018).

---

[9] Additional information is available at https://prepareforyourcare.org/welcome (accessed December 9, 2020).

[10] Additional information is available at https://acpdecisions.org (accessed December 9, 2020).

[11] Additional information is available at https://planwellguide.com (accessed December 10, 2020).

[12] Additional information is available at https://theconversationproject.org/nhdd/advance-care-planning (accessed December 9, 2020).

Sudore pointed out that questions remain concerning what the outcomes for ACP should be. "Is the outcome of completing an advance directive enough?" she asked. "Is goal-concordant care reasonable given the very well-known measurement challenges of this outcome?" A Delphi panel that focused on defining outcomes for successful ACP concluded that although the panelists considered goal-concordant care to be the "Holy Grail," they also acknowledged the difficulty in measuring that outcome as well as how focusing on that outcome could set the field up for failure (Sudore et al., 2018a).

In light of the mixed prior findings from many low-quality studies and systematic reviews, Sudore and her colleagues completed a scoping review of 69 high-quality ACP randomized trials from 2010 to 2020, none of which had been included in any prior reviews (McMahan et al., 2020). The review found that results of the primary outcomes from all ACP intervention types, including written materials, videos, and websites, were consistently positive. Specifically, the review revealed increased patient and surrogate satisfaction with communication and medical care and decreased surrogate and clinician distress, outcomes known to be important to patients. Despite these findings, the review found little or no evidence to support improved health status outcomes (such as quality of life) and quality-of-care outcomes (such as goal-concordant care) (McMahan et al., 2020).

Sudore noted the complexity of issues related to ACP, such as how the process can mean different things to different people depending on the context, creates uncertainty as to what precisely is needed to improve ACP. She suggested that new definitions might be needed to address context, life course, timing, and stakeholders. "I think we very much need patient and caregiver input on these definitions," said Sudore. She also encouraged consideration of the outcomes that one could reasonably expect from ACP, given that the process is but one small part of a broader, complex, and fragmented health care system. Sudore reiterated that because ACP is not owned by one specialty, program, or service line, no one group may be committed to moving it forward or studying successful clinical workflows.

In closing, Sudore pointed out that the differing perspectives on ACP present an opportunity to normalize the process across disciplines and the community. Sudore ended her remarks with a question to the audience: "Should ACP programs be taking a broader, more holistic approach where we use rigorous implementation science research principles in considering multiple stakeholders, context, culture, and workflows?"

## Discussion

To open the discussion session, moderator JoAnne Reifsnyder, executive vice president of clinical operations and chief nursing officer of Genesis HealthCare, returned to the two presenters who shared their lived experiences and asked Stuart and Harris how patient advocacy can help people understand and embrace the importance of talking about what matters to them with the people who matter. Harris replied that patient advocates have to regularly repeat that message over and over again to get people to realize that ACP is an important process in which to engage. Stuart added that the personal stories that patient advocates bring to the table can be a powerful spark to start the dialogue that people need to have with their loved ones.

When asked if she or her family members understood the terminology when first introduced to it, Stuart said her family did not have a good grasp of what ACP meant and who was supposed to implement the plan. While she knew what had to be done, it was difficult having the conversation with her father, so she tried to pay attention as best she could to the things he would mention as important. Harris said her husband did not understand the context for ACP, but he did understand the importance of the two of them making decisions before it was too late. Drawing from her 15-year experience as a health care professional and case manager working with ACP, Harris commented on the importance of explaining concepts and contexts in small pieces; she recounted how one patient thought a living will was designed to allow her son to take her money.

Reifsnyder asked Lo to comment on a February 2020 New Hampshire Supreme Court ruling[13] that "appears to prioritize best interests over substituted judgment." Lo replied that on one hand, it does not make sense to talk about substituted judgments—where the proxy will make a decision that they know or think their loved one would make if they could decide for themselves—if a patient who is unable to communicate their wishes has not previously addressed a particular issue or given an indication of core values from which a non-family member or designated caregiver can extrapolate. On the other hand, in some situations involving the patients who understand what is about to happen to them, doing what the patient said makes sense.

---

[13] Additional information is available at https://law.justia.com/cases/new-hampshire/supreme-court/2020/2018-0701.html (accessed December 9, 2020).

Responding to a question about intermediate goals that could measure success in achieving goal-concordant care, Sudore said that is what everyone wants, but it is hard to measure because the situation at the bedside can change at the last minute. "From the scoping review and what we are hearing from patients and surrogates, some of the most important outcomes are about surrogate burden," she explained, "and some studies are showing decreased moral distress [for clinicians]." In her opinion, those are good proxies for whether things went as well as they could have. "Some of that could have been from great advance care planning, some could have been the result of having wonderful clinicians at the bedside, or a combination of both," she added.

Lo commented that one challenge that dementia and cognitive impairment creates is that the patient is no longer the individual that people remember. Sudore added that just because someone is cognitively impaired does not necessarily mean that they do not have the capacity to make certain decisions. In fact, she and her colleagues have found that people with mild to moderate cognitive impairment can engage in the Prepare for Your Care program and consistently have the necessary conversations about their values.

Given Sudore's research, which has shown that a key motivating factor driving patients to complete an advance care plan is to alleviate the burden on surrogate decision makers and that ACP appears to reduce that burden, Reifsnyder asked Sudore if those factors have changed the way she thinks about the Prepare for Your Care program. Sudore replied that the program was meant to be a step-by-step process that can be completed with an individual's surrogate, so recent research has only emphasized the importance of having these conversations with surrogates. In fact, The Greenwall Foundation is funding Sudore's efforts to create surrogate preparation modules for the program. She added that she and her colleagues are now attempting to include surrogate outcomes in their research studies.

## INTERPRETING THE EVIDENCE BASE FOR ADVANCE CARE PLANNING

### What Is the Evidence and Why Does It Matter?

Opening the workshop's second session, Sean Morrison, professor of geriatrics and palliative medicine at the Icahn School of Medicine at Mount Sinai, gave a brief overview of the history of ACP and discussed the evidence and why it matters in the context of achieving the quest for goal-concordant care. He reiterated the Delphi definition shared earlier by Sudore: ACP is "a process that supports adults at any age or stage of health in understanding and sharing their personal values, life goals, and preferences regarding future medical care" (Sudore et al., 2017). Morrison added that "the goal is to make sure that people receive care that is consistent with their values, goals, and preferences during serious and chronic illness. And for many people, this is going to include choosing and preparing a trusted person to make decisions for them in the event that they lose decisional capacity." This is different, he said, from having real-time discussions about real-time decisions or in-the-moment discussions around goals of care either with patients or with proxies. "I think all of us would agree that it is critically important that we do this every single day, but that it is not advance care planning. There is no 'advance' in that care planning," he added.

Morrison noted, as Lo stated in the first session, that ACP has a long, complicated history beginning in the 1960s when patients were receiving unwanted treatments at the end of life, which led to the first living will in 1967. The realization that it is impossible to predict all treatment decisions that might arise led to the idea that if a person could not state specifically what treatments they would want in the future, perhaps they could designate a trusted individual to make those decisions. The result was the advent of the health care proxy or durable power of attorney, which California first signed into law in 1983 (Sabatino, 2010). According to Morrison, the challenge then became one of engaging reluctant physicians to have the necessary conversations with their patients, which led to the proliferation of ACP programs that did not require a physician office visit or physician–patient interaction.

Unfortunately, Morrison remarked, research indicated that even when patients documented their preferences and named their proxies, providers were not acting on those preferences. This realization, said Morrison, led to Oregon creating the physician orders for life-sustaining treatment (POLST) form in 1991, which translated patient and family preferences into actionable physician orders. However, physicians were still not engaging in ACP discussions and not completing POLST forms, which put pressure on Medicare to provide reimbursement for ACP conversations.

Morrison noted, though, that some patients who have completed a POLST form are not aware they have done so or even what the form contains. He added that many patients who came to the hospital during the COVID-19 pandemic and had POLST forms in their electronic health records (EHRs) disagreed with what was on them and instead opted for treatments that saved their lives. "We also saw that the simple presence of a POLST form during the COVID-19 pandemic discouraged many of our providers from having complex discussions because they simply did not have time and it was easier just to look at the form," he said.

Turning to the evidence base for ACP, Morrison noted that although many of the studies have been of low quality, $30 million in federal funding has been spent on ACP research in the past 30 years (Morrison, 2020). This research includes randomized controlled trials (RCTs) of more than 16,000 individuals and the scoping review of 69 studies (McMahan et al., 2020) discussed earlier. That evidence, said Morrison, suggests that advance directives are a reasonable surrogate for a completed ACP discussion, be it for a treatment directive or designation of a health care proxy. He added that the prevalence of advance directives increased from 26 percent in 1993 to 37 percent in 2016, but in 2020—30 years after the Patient Self-Determination Act—less than half of U.S. residents have one (Knight et al., 2020; Waller et al., 2019).

Morrison explained that researchers have studied adults of all ages: healthy, hospitalized, in critical care, living in the community, living in nursing homes, and with multiple different diseases. "We have looked at attitudes, beliefs, and preference, and what we hear consistently from the public is that this is something that they would want and they would want their physician to discuss with them," said Morrison. Investigators have also examined numerous interventions, including patient education and decision support; physician, nurse, and social worker education and reminders; nurse, social worker, and physician-led group and individual counseling; and individual or group counseling provided by a trained advance care facilitator.

Morrison noted the many positive findings from the preponderance of evidence, such as that these interventions improve people's knowledge about ACP and increase the completion of advance directives (Jimenez et al., 2018). Data suggest that these interventions can also increase documentation and even the rate of ACP discussions with physicians if it is measured immediately after the intervention (Jimenez et al., 2018). Morrison noted, however, that little is known about the long-term effects of these interventions. Moreover, Morrison said, high-quality studies offer minimal to no consistent evidence that ACP can (1) influence medical care at the end of life for patients lacking decisional capacity, (2) enhance the quality of death and dying, (3) increase the likelihood that end-of-life care is consistent with patient preferences, (4) improve patient or surrogate satisfaction, or (5) improve surrogate quality of life or bereavement outcomes.

In Morrison's view, researchers have been unable to find conclusive evidence that ACP works to achieve its main outcomes, due in part to the reality that the health care system must be organized to respond in ways that are consistent with the values and goals that were identified through the ACP process, wherein patients are able to articulate their values and goals and identify which treatments would align with those goals in hypothetical future scenarios. Morrison said,

> Clinicians need to honor those preferences and decisions, and our health system and the society at large that we work in [needs to] be able to support that goal-concordant care—so that if somebody calls 911 in the middle of the night and says "my husband is in terrible pain but does not want to go to the hospital," somebody will come and be able to manage that pain rather than having to call 911 for assistance, and if we [can] do all this, patients will receive goal-concordant care.

However, one complication is that treatment choices near the end of life are not simple, logical, linear, autonomous, or predictable. Rather, said Morrison, they are complex, uncertain, socially determined, emotional, and malleable depending on the clinical situation. Moreover, Morrison remarked that substituted judgment presumes that surrogates can do three things:

1. Extrapolate specific treatment decisions from distant general ACP discussions;
2. Piece together what their loved one would have wanted; and
3. Disentangle their own preferences, emotions, and feelings of guilt from the decision.

Morrison further noted that treatment decisions do not occur in a vacuum; they are driven by financial incentives and the marketplace. "We know that supply and demand influence the care that people receive in the setting of serious illness," he said, "and that [treatment decisions] are influenced by our societal capacity to support patient needs and are strongly influenced by regional cultures and practice patterns."

Morrison remarked that continuing to invest in ACP is not benign and does have consequences. For example, the poor communication skills that often characterize ACP practices can lead to goal-discordant and suboptimal care (Heyland et al., 2006; IOM, 2015; You et al., 2015). Morrison said that merely varying the language used in ACP can change treatment decisions.

He added that treatment or surrogate decisions are strongly influenced by how choices are framed, and the lack of quality control around most discussions can lead to withholding beneficial treatments (Heyland, 2020).

Morrison concluded his remarks with a question: "Why is there such strong faith in the premise of ACP despite 30 years of evidence to the contrary? I could argue that if we had this evidence base in any other area of medicine, we would not be continuing." He listed several possible reasons:

- Respect for the individual and a belief that ACP matters,
- The uniquely Western belief in individualism,
- Commitment bias (the field is so committed to making this work that there is no vision for a different way forward),
- Confirmation bias (finding positive results and ignoring the negative results),
- Financial incentives that reimburse clinicians for having ACP discussions, and
- An industry that has developed to support and promote ACP as a result of the lack of available alternate approaches.

In closing, Morrison wondered if a more productive approach would be to narrow the focus of these efforts to simply having everyone appoint a health care proxy. "I would argue that the preponderance of evidence suggests that the long and winding road of ACP should end," said Morrison.

> Perhaps, as Dr. Sudore pointed out, we should be focusing on how to better prepare [patients and families] to have these conversations. Perhaps we should be thinking about how to better guide surrogates through in-the-moment decision making and how to have real-time communication about real-time decisions rather than focusing our effort on something that, for the most part, just has not shown great benefit.

## How Clinical and Health Care Leaders Use Advance Care Planning Research

Carole Montgomery, executive medical director of Respecting Choices, explained that she would not be speaking from the perspective of a researcher, but rather of a clinical care leader who is a consumer of the research on ACP. She added that she would address how that research can inform and guide the work that she and other executives do in real-life settings with organizations and communities that aim to improve the standard of care for everyone. Referring to the earlier discussions, Montgomery noted that the maturing definition of ACP has occurred in the context of other changes in health care, including the growth and development of palliative care as a recognized medical specialty and the movement toward person-centered care as a pillar of quality. The person-centered care movement, added Montgomery, was influenced by consumerism and calls for transparency, which has driven a shift in the perspective that patients can and should play a role in the decision-making process about their care and treatment. Moreover, clinicians have had to accept that knowing a patient's goals and values can and should change their role in the decision-making process. This attitudinal evolution has occurred within the greater context of a health care system that is increasingly complex and fragmented, said Montgomery. "With all of this shifting in the surrounding milieu of health care, it is no wonder that it is a significant challenge to interpret the mixed history of evidence around ACP," she said.

In that context, said Montgomery, the scoping review that Sudore discussed (McMahan et al., 2020) is an important body of work that adds to the evidence base for ACP and addresses the deficiencies of prior systematic reviews by including only RCTs from the past decade. Sudore's review also accurately reflected the variety of research occurring in the ACP realm, including research that tested different interventions enacted across a variety of populations, in different settings, and at various times in the trajectory of life and illness, said Montgomery. All told, the 69 reviewed studies encompassed 170 different outcomes and teased out which outcomes were most often affected across all the studies that examined those outcomes.

Before reviewing these outcomes, Montgomery stressed that the ultimate stakeholders in this work—patients, their surrogates, and family members—have already weighed in on the ACP outcomes that matter most to them; based on patients' lived experiences, they want to be involved in their care and decisions (Guyatt et al., 2004). "They want to talk with their medical team about ACP to help prepare them for decision making, and they see ACP as a way for preparing their families and surrogate decision makers, decreasing their loved ones' decision-making burden, and ultimately ensuring that their own wishes are honored," said Montgomery (Curtis et al., 2001; Sessanna and Jezewski, 2008; Sharp et al., 2013; Singer et al., 1999; Steinhauser et al., 2000; Sudore et al., 2020; Wenrich et al., 2001).

Montgomery noted that the majority of the recent high-quality RCTs evaluated in the scoping review showed significant effects of those very same patient-desired outcomes. For example, 72 percent of the studies evaluating process outcomes of ACP revealed improvements in patient readiness, confidence, and self-efficacy. Similarly, 86 percent of the studies evaluating action outcomes found increased completion of ACP conversations, discussions with family, or creation of ACP documentations; 88 percent found congruence between a patient's goals, values, and beliefs and their surrogate's or clinician's understanding; and 100 percent found that patients, surrogates, and clinicians were satisfied with those communications. All of the studies that examined the health impact on surrogates saw reduced depression, anxiety, posttraumatic stress disorder (PTSD), and complex grief (McMahan et al., 2020).

In terms of goal-concordant care, Montgomery said she believes that if this work is done correctly, goal-concordant care should be hard to measure. As she explained,

> Patients want help to prepare for making decisions in the future, not to make decisions prematurely for a future hypothetical event, so they and their surrogates will be ready to participate as equal partners in that decision making when that future unpredictable, complex situation arises, because that is the moment when treatment preferences are put into context, and goal-concordant care either does or does not occur. It is not something where a static goal can be recorded in advance against which future care is then graded.

In Montgomery's view, surrogates' satisfaction with the communication involved in decision making and whether they experience less of a burden in making decisions are all appropriate proxy measures for goal-concordant care. In that respect, Montgomery believes that the scoping review (McMahan et al., 2020) helped show that ACP has a significant, positive effect on the outcomes that matter most to patients and their surrogates.

Montgomery said she is encouraged that recent studies are incorporating more diverse populations, but she cautioned that it does not mean that all populations are sharing the achieved outcomes equally. She argued that in general, health care must aim to become more trustworthy, and preparing individuals and their loved ones to engage in health care decision making could be a first step toward that goal. In fact, she said, recent research indicates that ACP is accomplishing that goal among diverse populations. For example, one study used the Respecting Choices intervention with HIV-positive urban adult populations and found that ACP improved treatment preference congruence between patients and their surrogates, an understanding that persisted even as the patients' treatment preferences changed (Lyon et al., 2020). Two other studies found that the Prepare for Your Care intervention achieved a higher level of engagement in ACP among diverse

English- and Spanish-speaking older adults (Sudore et al., 2020) and among those with limited health literacy or who spoke only Spanish (Freytag et al., 2020). Montgomery pointed out, however, that if preparing individuals to engage as equal partners in health care is a first step toward becoming trustworthy, completing that journey requires embracing the shift in power at the point of decision making and having clinicians accept that they cannot know the right care to deliver without knowing what matters most to the person for whom they are caring.

In closing, Montgomery acknowledged the value of practice-based evidence that emerges from shared experiences, clinical examples, and expertise developed during clinical practice. She emphasized the important role that implementation science plays in examining what works, for whom, and under what circumstances, as well as in determining how to adapt and scale effective interventions in ways that are accessible, equitable, and able to confirm the strategies that work. In that regard, she argued that pragmatic trials should have a significant role in future ACP research because they are better able to measure and evaluate the challenges of an evolving complex process across various stakeholders and in real-life situations. "This should be our path forward to achieve what we know patients and surrogates want and to continue on the journey to becoming trustworthy partners in their care," concluded Montgomery.

## Making Sense of the Evidence

Daren Heyland, professor of internal medicine and critical care at the Queen's University School of Medicine in Kingston, Canada, began by noting that as a critical care clinician, he has witnessed a significant amount of suffering when people come into an intensive care environment ill prepared for decision making and ultimately do not always receive the care that is right for them. "If the goal of ACP is to try and increase person-centered care, increase goal-concordant care, or increase the process of communication in decision making around the use or non-use of life-sustaining treatments, I think we have a long way to go," said Heyland.

To support that statement, Heyland referred to several studies showing that patient and family wishes are not always followed—even with an advance care plan. For example, one study of elderly patients in the ICU on life support found that 25 percent of the families had stated a preference for only "comfort measures" (Heyland et al., 2016), while another study found that of the patients who preferred to forgo cardiopulmonary resuscitation

(CPR), 35 percent had orders in their medical records to receive it (Heyland et al., 2015). Moreover, a study of clinician–family communication found that 26 percent of family conferences did not address patient values and preferences, and only 8 percent of decisions were based on these (Scheunemann et al., 2019).

Heyland noted that in the evidence base supporting ACP, there is tremendous heterogeneity in terms of the intervention and how the investigators conceptualized it, the populations studied, the case mix, and the patients' life journeys (McMahan et al., 2020). "Our valuation of this corpus of data might be a bit dependent upon which piece or pieces of that heterogeneous body of data we examine carefully," said Heyland. The key point, he continued, is that that body of data is too heterogeneous to make meaningful conclusions. "I do not think it is fair to say that ACP works or does not work," noted Heyland. To make such a determination, "we need to move to a higher degree of granularity or homogeneity that includes standardization about what works and what does not work."

Heyland also expressed concern about the current definition and conceptual framework for ACP, given that planning for death under conditions of certainty is not the same as planning for serious illness under conditions of uncertainty. Additionally, he cautioned that decontextualized planning conversations can be equated with medical decisions. "The current approach, where we rely heavily on conversation and open-ended questions that elicit values and preferences, is also problematic and may explain why there is still quite a bit of medical error in this space," said Heyland. Heyland cautioned that people are not always informed consumers; it is often not as simple as asking them what they want.

One problem with ACP as it is currently practiced, explained Heyland, is that most care plans are framed around the end of life. What happens, he asked, when someone is short of breath and the critical care clinicians are trying to decide to use or withhold life-sustaining treatments? "I do not know if you are dying, so what validity do plans have when made under the context of 'if I am dying, this is what I want or do not want' when applied to a different context when there is no certainty that this is your final episode?" He noted that research on the use of POLST has shown that more than one-third of the time, patients receive care in the ICU that is not concordant with their wishes (Heyland, 2020). "Is this a problem with us, or it is a problem with the tool that focuses on end-of-life care?" he asked.

Heyland pointed out that another way of conceptualizing ACP is by the tasks that ultimately lead to ordering life-sustaining treatments (see

*26    THE CHALLENGES AND OPPORTUNITIES OF ADVANCE CARE PLANNING*

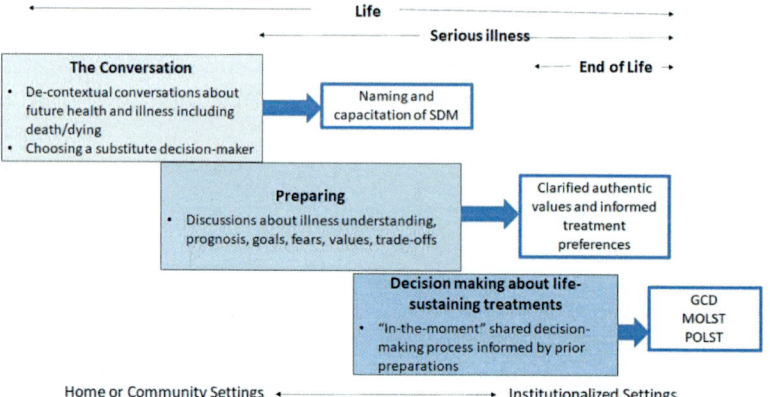

**FIGURE 2** The continuum of communication and decision making in serious illness care.
NOTE: GCD = goal-concordant decision making; MOLST = medical orders for life-sustaining treatment; POLST = physician orders for life-sustaining treatment; SDM = substitute decision maker.
SOURCE: Daren Heyland presentation, October 26, 2020.

Figure 2). This approach does not skip the step of preparing the patient with discussions about their illness; their prognosis; their fears, goals, and values; and the trade-offs that come with any decision. He also believed that the current ACP process violates legal provisions intended to protect the informed consent process, which is designed to explain risks, benefits, and possible outcomes as part of the thorough discussion that leads to shared decision making. Instead, he argued for focusing on better preparing patients and surrogate decision makers to make decisions in the moment, rather than using a document that has limited validity and clinical utility to make such decisions in advance (Heyland, 2020; Sudore and Fried, 2010).

Heyland explained that he and his colleagues have researched whether people are able to express their authentic values and informed treatment preferences, and the results indicate they are not (Heyland et al., 2017). "Those value statements [people] make are sometimes in conflict with other things that come out of their mouth as another expression of value and bear no relationship to what might be the treatment preference," he explained. For example, the statement "live as long as possible" correlated positively with a seemingly contradictory statement of "be comfortable and suffer as little as possible." As a result, clinicians are left trying to interpret what a value statement means and how it connects to a medical order to use or forgo life-sustaining treatments (You et al., 2015). That process, in Heyland's view, is irreproducible, nontransparent, and an explanation for why so much medical error exists. It also argues for the need for more decision-making support if the goal is to ground people's care in their individual values and preferences, he added.

For this reason, Heyland noted that he and his colleagues have shifted from planning for death to an approach that helps people think about serious illness, provides more sophisticated tools using constrained values, and uses a decision aid that highlights the difference among ICU care, medical care, and comfort care. Compared to other ACP tools, their program, called the Plan Well Guide:

- discriminates between planning for terminal care versus planning for serious illness,
- explains how clinicians make medical decisions under conditions of uncertainty,
- uses a constrained values clarification tool where respondents must pick between competing values,
- uses grids to transparently connect stated values to respondent preferences for medical treatments during serious illness, and
- provides a first-in-class decision aid on the different levels of care (Heyland et al., 2020).

Heyland noted that an RCT (Heyland et al., 2020) revealed that the Plan Well Guide increased the likelihood of patients receiving the care that is right for them (as determined by the constrained value clarification tools and elicited through the guide) and reduced decision conflict. In addition, clinicians in the study reported spending less time finalizing the goals of care with patients who received the intervention compared to usual care. Moreover, the study demonstrated that the majority of patients and surrogates were quite satisfied with the experience and would recommend it to others.

Based on these results, Heyland suggested a new paradigm, which he called Advance Serious Illness Preparation and Planning (see Figure 3). In this paradigm, most activities focus on preparing people to be able to express their authentic values and informed treatment preferences in the moment using more sophisticated tools and decision aids.

Heyland concluded his presentation by reiterating his belief that the way forward is to shift from the current approach framed around making

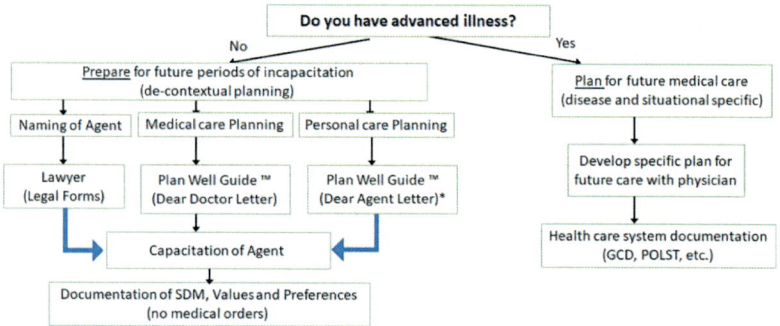

**FIGURE 3** Advanced serious illness preparation and planning.
NOTES: *The Dear Agent Letter has yet to be developed. GCD = goal-concordant decision making; POLST = physician orders for life-sustaining treatment; SDM = substitute decision maker.
SOURCE: Daren Heyland presentation, October 26, 2020.

treatment decisions in advance for end-of-life care to an approach that aims to provide optimal, person-centered medical care for people with serious illness in situations of uncertainty about whether they are experiencing the end of life.

### Advance Care Planning Is a Right: A Medical–Legal Perspective

The session's final speaker, Patricia Bomba, vice president and medical director of geriatrics at Excellus BlueCross BlueShield, began by thanking Stuart and Harris for providing important real-world context for the workshop speakers' presentations by sharing their lived experiences. Referring to Lo's earlier description of the Patient Self-Determination Act, Bomba concluded that everyone has a right to make medical decisions throughout their lifetime—including at the end of life.

Bomba explained that over the 40 years that she has been a practicing geriatrician, she has seen medical care shift from a paternalistic model, where physicians made all of the decisions, to an autonomous model that expects patients to make decisions. The desired state, in Bomba's view, is one of shared decision making but also acknowledges that in-the-moment decisions in the ICU or ED are often complicated by the fact that many individuals lack the capacity to decide for themselves. Bomba briefly recounted a few stories that illustrate the value of ACP. One couple prepared in advance for the end of life, reducing the burden on the surrogate and family, while another individual thought he had all the time in the world, did not prepare, and left his wife and niece to suffer through more than 3 months of seeing their loved one on life support. Bomba shared that in the latter case, the family members struggled for years with the decisions they had made. Rather than abandoning ACP, in Bomba's view, it is important to continue working toward a culture change that integrates ACP and health care planning in the same way that legal planning and financial planning have already been well integrated into everyday life.

Bomba noted that in the United States, all 50 states have their own forms and public health laws regarding end-of-life decisions. In New York, for example, Bomba explained that ACP has evolved in a way that aligns with the Delphi definition presented at the start of the workshop. New York has taken a population health approach in which advance directives focus specifically on choosing the appropriate health care agent identified in the health care proxy, with living wills being less of a focus, as these are difficult to interpret due to the coexistence of potentially reversible disease and end-stage irreversible illness. Bomba pointed out that medical orders for life-sustaining treatment (MOLST) is a set of medical orders created after a thoughtful discussion that focuses on life-sustaining treatment preferences for individuals who have advanced illness or frailty, such as resuscitation preference, respiratory support, and hospitalization transfers. Underscoring that this is a continuous process, Bomba noted that what someone values at age 18 is different from what they value at 81 and is certainly different in the last year of their life. In Bomba's view, Community Conversations on Compassionate Care (CCCC)[14] is an example of an ACP program for the general population 18 years and older that aligns with the Delphi definition. Bomba explained that the program emphasizes learning about decision making, sharing values and beliefs, and choosing the appropriate trusted person to serve as a health care agent.

Bomba noted that New York's CCCC program, which the state has been using since 2001, doubled the percentage of people preparing health care proxies from 20 to 42 percent in upstate New York by 2008 (Bomba and Orem, 2015). Bomba pointed out that virtually every state is now working on developing this type of program for those who might die in the next year, are living in a nursing home or receiving long-term services at

---

[14] Additional information is available at https://compassionandsupport.org/advance-care-planning/cccc (accessed December 10, 2020).

home, or are near the end of life. Noting the many studies about POLST form completion and goal-concordant care, she highlighted one study of nursing home residents that found that completed POLST comfort care orders are strongly associated with fewer treatments compared to situations without a completed POLST form or a form calling for full treatment (Hickman et al., 2010). A study conducted in a hospital setting found similar results (Lee et al., 2020).

Bomba noted that completing the MOLST form requires a thoughtful discussion in order to achieve goal concordance. New York uses seven checklists to ensure compliance with the ethical and legal requirements for end-of-life decisions and a standard MOLST protocol consisting of the following eight steps (Bomba, 2005, revised 2011):

1. Prepare for discussion
   - Understand the patient's health status, prognosis, and ability to consent
   - Retrieve completed advance directives
   - Determine decision maker and public health law legal requirements
2. Determine what the patient/family know
3. Explore goals, hopes, and expectations
4. Suggest realistic goals
5. Respond empathetically
6. Use MOLST to guide choices and finalize patient wishes
   - Engage in shared, informed medical decision making
   - Undertake conflict resolution
7. Complete and sign MOLST
   - Follow public health law and document conversation
8. Review and revise periodically

This multi-step process, said Bomba, ensures that MOLST is completed properly and that patients, families, and clinicians are prepared for the end-of-life discussion. She added that New York has three public health laws and a process laid out by the Surrogate's Court Procedure Act 1705B[15] that governs decisions for those who have intellectual or developmental disabilities and lack decision-making capacity.

---

[15] For more information, see https://codes.findlaw.com/ny/surrogates-court-procedure-act/scp-sect-1705.html (accessed December 10, 2020).

According to Bomba, a key lesson learned has been the importance of screening for appropriate populations; assessing capacity, given that people may still have the ability to make decisions; and making sure that people understand their health status and prognosis before they think about their goals for care. Bomba noted that developing a palliative care plan to ensure that pain and symptom management is available at all times and that the caregivers receive support is also important.

New York has developed a secure website[16] to serve as an online MOLST completion system and a registry, which is person centered and meets all of the legal requirements spelled out by state law. She further explained that the website can integrate with the major EHRs and health information exchanges, including HealthX.[17] In Bomba's view, the website has improved the quality of care, as well as patient safety, and it provides access to completed MOLST forms during an emergency. Bomba added that it also promotes coordinated, person-centered care by improving workflow within and across facilities. She shared that, as of September 30, 2020, approximately 50,000 live patients, with a mean age of 82 and a median age of 85, have completed forms in the registry. Eighty-two percent expressed their preference for not wanting to be resuscitated, 72 percent did not want to be intubated, and 21 percent stated they did not want to be hospitalized. During the COVID-19 pandemic, 20 percent of the individuals reviewed and renewed their MOLST orders (Excellus BlueCross BlueShield, 2020).

In closing, Bomba explained that working with community partners on culture change and moving upstream with the appropriate populations in the state's clinical practices has helped New York avoid some of the pitfalls that other speakers discussed. "We know we need to choose a trusted person, foster culture change, build patient-centered systems, and establish metrics that are different for the general population regarding advance directives versus medical orders," said Bomba. "The bottom line is it is complex but it is right, and we ought to be measuring what matters most to patients and families."

## Discussion

Discussion session moderator Susan E. Hickman, director of the Indiana University Center for Aging Research at the Regenstrief Institute,

---

[16] See https://www.nysemolstregistry.com (accessed December 10, 2020).
[17] For more information, see https://www.healthx.com (accessed December 10, 2020).

opened the discussion by asking Montgomery if she believes that early ACP is appropriate, and if so, under what circumstances. Montgomery replied that she fully supports the process definition of ACP because it talks about supporting all adults at any stage so they understand and share what matters to them. For Montgomery, talking about what some might call "upstream" ACP (as opposed to "just-in-time" planning) helps prepare individuals for making informed, thoughtful decisions and is useful precisely because serious illness is not always predictable. However, she added, the conversations in early ACP need to cover different content and probably have a different ending than those for an individual preparing for the end of life, when those decisions are more proximal. Montgomery added that she believes it is problematic to wait to introduce ACP only for those with serious illness. Doing so, in her view, puts clinicians in control of when to engage a patient more fully, which she said is disrespectful to individuals and their families.

Hickman asked Heyland to contemplate what is needed from the field to build on recent conceptual and methodological research. Heyland responded by citing a gap in the research in terms of how much clinicians help people develop their authentic value statements. "If you think about how much the research enterprise invests in measurement of patient-reported outcomes or quality-of-care metrics or quality-of-life metrics, we still ground important clinical decisions on patient values," he said, "but where is the research and methodological development that helps us make sure that we are actually measuring something that is reproducible, something that is valid, something that is predictable or translatable into a clinical action?"

Another research gap that Heyland identified is in the area of decision aids, noted Hickman. Heyland remarked that a growing body of work shows that these aids support people with serious illness, helping them make better decisions. He emphasized that despite the existence of decision aids, implementation has lagged behind, resulting in people making decisions without having access to tools known to work.

When asked about his view of the different findings from the older review of lower-quality studies and the more recent review of RCTs, Morrison noted that, in his view, it was disrespectful to those who conducted the earlier studies to simply ignore them. That said, "when you look at the randomized controlled high-quality studies and you look at what they were designed to do … overwhelmingly, when you look at those results, the main outcomes were negative," explained Morrison, even though what people cite are the positive results. He added that in most cases, researchers were focusing on secondary outcomes that the studies were not designed to address; he attributed this disconnect to confirmation bias. Overall, in Morrison's view, it is time to think about how to better guide people in their decision making at the time when they need to make decisions, not when thinking about hypothetical events.

Hickman asked Morrison if he was suggesting that clinicians not talk to patients about their goals and values ahead of time, even when using a model such as the one Heyland presented. Morrison clarified that he was arguing for not focusing time, effort, and money on conversations with people who may not experience serious illness for many years. "That is different from having a real-time, goals-of-care discussion about something that matters right now," said Morrison.

Montgomery explained that she was not intending to convey the idea of disregarding studies simply because they were conducted decades ago. Rather, she said, it is important to understand the massive change that has gone on in health care in the 30 years since that research was conducted. Montgomery compared differing perspectives on ACP with the process of discharge planning, which was once thought to be a simple, singular event at a point in time with a clear owner and individual accountability. "Now we understand that as one piece of a complex process we now refer to as 'transition of care' and consider in a more holistic way," she said.

Heyland clarified that what he and Morrison were arguing is that effort, energy, and further research should be devoted to better preparing people for in-the-moment clinical decisions and that having laypeople, even seriously ill people, make decisions in advance that are expected to be followed in the future risks leading to medical error.

Bomba emphasized the importance of the ACP process and said those with serious illness and advanced frailty need to have the opportunity, before they lose capacity, to weigh in on the decisions regarding their end-of-life care. To be able to do that requires ensuring that, over time, they have honest conversations about what matters most to them and are able to share that information with their health care agent or surrogate, as well as their family, as living and dying are both family events. In addition, she said, it is important that when someone gets to the place where their physicians would not be surprised if they died in the next year, that they are not making decisions without understanding their health status and prognosis. "If they think they have 10 years of life and they really are hospice eligible, their decision-making process would be different," said Bomba.

Bomba shared that she uses four questions to guide her discussions with seriously ill patients. Will the treatment make a difference? What are the benefits and burdens; in other words, will the treatment help or hurt? Is there hope of getting better and, if so, what will life be like afterward? What do you value and what is important to you? "I think is incumbent on us to make sure we are answering those questions in thoughtful ways that help people make decisions," she said.

Hickman, noting that Heyland had observed that terminally ill patients can make medical decisions in advance for future life-limiting complications in consultation with their clinicians, asked him if he sees a role for advance directives and POLST for people with life-limiting serious illness who are at risk of life-threatening clinical events. Noting that he did see a role, Heyland cautioned that the challenge is that those decisions are often made without the clinician who is involved in the actual in-the-moment decision making. "Imagine the scenario of a patient I saw with advanced cancer with a prescribed living will that said if 'I'm dying, no heroics,' but they present with heart failure. Do they know that with 24 hours of positive-pressure ventilation and a squirt of Lasix, I could get them back to how they were, still with a several-months' trajectory of life?" stated Heyland. "I cannot cope with the uncertainty of what they knew, what they did not know, and how informed and comprehensive their conversation was." He noted that the default in critical care is to intubate and sort it out later, which to him is a failure in the planning process. His preference is to shift away from making these treatment decisions in advance and instead codify values and preferences while recognizing that health care providers have to go through an informed consent process with the patient, if they are able when the appropriate time arrives, or with a substitute.

Bomba noted that medical orders, such as a completed POLST form, are not one-and-done decisions; they need to be reviewed and potentially modified in light of a change in health status, and serve as the basis for medical orders to be followed in an emergency. Heyland countered that real-time audits of real-time practice show that the POLST form is often used as an excuse to not have a conversation with a surrogate. "If there was a mistake in what was codified under one context and there is no conversation with the substitute, then medical errors are being committed," he explained. Bomba replied that this is where a system like New York's eMOLST can prove useful, as it documents the conversation and the accompanying medical orders.

On a final note, Hickman asked Bomba to comment on how the COVID-19 pandemic has changed the thinking about ACP and elevated its importance. Bomba reiterated that the online system she spoke about saw 20 percent of the completed MOLST forms reviewed and renewed due to the pandemic. Bomba noted that New York's eMOLST users also reported that patients wanted to have additional conversations with their clinicians and perhaps change their eMOLST orders in light of COVID-19 and their current health status.

## A BRIEF SUMMARY OF THE FIRST WEBINAR

To open the second session, Hickman provided a brief summary of the discussions from the first session. She first thanked the two volunteers from NPAF, Stuart and Harris, who generously shared personal stories of their experiences caring for loved ones through the course of serious illness and the end of life. Hickman noted that although both women discussed ways in which the health care system had failed them, they concluded that proactive conversations about goals, values, and preferences, while difficult, are incredibly important.

Hickman noted that Lo and Sudore provided a grounding framework for understanding the historical context of ACP and its evolution out of landmark case law, as well as significant advancements in developing consensus about how to define ACP and measure outcomes. The two presented the consensus definition for ACP as agreed upon by an international Delphi panel: "[a] process that supports adults at any age or stage of health in understanding and sharing their personal values, life goals and preferences regarding future medical care" (Sudore et al., 2017). This definition, said Hickman, helps move ACP away from focusing only on documents and treatment decisions toward actually preparing people for communication and in-the-moment decision making.

The second session of the first part of the webinar focused on different interpretations of the evidence for ACP, followed by what Hickman characterized as a "spirited" discussion. Summarizing the key takeaways from that session, Hickman noted that the evidence base for ACP is equivocal because of significant quality issues in past research (Jimenez et al., 2018). In addition, though prior high-quality studies exist, these were often based on old conceptualizations of ACP, and as the field has matured, it has developed a broad recognition that the earlier conceptualizations do not capture the full complexity of ACP. Hickman explained that this complexity includes factors such as how the conversations may change based on patients' readiness and where they are in their life trajectory. Moreover, despite the many stakeholders involved in the ACP process—including patients, surrogate decision makers, the community, clinicians, health care systems, and policy makers—no single discipline or profession "owns" ACP. Another factor in the complexity of ACP, noted Hickman, involves understanding which outcomes are reasonable to expect, given that the "Holy Grail" of goal-concordant care may be hard to measure and that other outcomes, such as improved quality of life, may not be appropriate, particularly in a population nearing the end of life.

Increasingly, said Hickman, the field is developing consensus around measurement using meaningful, realistic outcomes. One recent review of 69 RCTs conducted over the past 10 years (McMahan et al., 2020) suggests positive outcomes in important areas, notably for decreased surrogate distress, an outcome that patients say is critically important to them. She noted that several of the panelists in this session argued that more research is direly needed in several areas:

- supporting patients and developing authentic value statements;
- using decision aids to support decision making in the course of serious illness;
- implementation science that accounts for local context and tailors interventions to the resources available in a given setting;
- informatics and online platforms, such as eMOLST, that can improve quality through standardized conversation elements, increased accessibility, and real-time updating; and
- pragmatic trials that aim to conduct science in the real world to overcome barriers that frequently prevent successful clinical trial outcomes from being widely implemented.

Hickman recounted differing opinions among the panelists about what constitutes ACP. One perspective argued that discussing goals of care in the context of making treatment decisions, which many consider to be part of informed consent, is distinct from ACP. A more broadly held view was that these activities often fall along the continuum of ACP interventions, ranging from identifying a surrogate to preparing patients for serious illness decision making. There was also disagreement about when patients with serious illness should be asked to engage in the ACP process. Some panelists argued that preparation for in-the-moment decision making should start well before a medical crisis occurs, while other panelists were in favor of a just-in-time communications model with clinicians instead. This panel also raised concerns about how these ACP models might not meet the needs of underserved and disadvantaged patients who lack access to health care, minority communities that have experienced systemic racism and therefore mistrust the system and clinicians, or people with dementia or cognitive impairments who are unable to express their preferences and are poorly served by just-in-time decisions.

The panelists did agree that evidence suggests advance directives alone are inadequate, Hickman summarized. They argued that early ACP should focus on identifying and preparing surrogates and identifying broad goals but in general should avoid treatment decisions, as it is difficult to anticipate the context in which these decisions will apply. The panelists also agreed that preparation is a key component of ACP and that clinicians need to know patients' values and goals to help support the best high-quality decision making.

Hickman concluded her summary by noting that

> despite the evolution of the field from end-of-life treatments and advance directives to a process of preparation for medical decision making, and despite the consensus definition that I started with that was created by the Delphi panel, there really were different opinions about what even constitutes ACP. It was discussed that the 2017 Delphi panel definition may need to be revisited and should include input from patients and caregivers to guide future research and practice.

In closing, Hickman pointed out that the panelists agreed that moving the field forward requires identifying the outcomes that the ACP process can reasonably be expected to produce and evaluating interventions in real-world settings that account for the complexity of ACP.

## THINKING DIFFERENTLY ABOUT ADVANCE CARE PLANNING

### Flaws in Advance Care Planning Implementation and Evaluation

Scott Halpern, director of the Palliative and Advanced Illness Research Center and the John M. Eisenberg Professor of Medicine, Epidemiology, and Medical Ethics and Health Policy at the University of Pennsylvania Perelman School of Medicine, began his presentation by noting that he agreed completely with Morrison's conclusion about the lack of consistent or solid evidence to support ACP. He pointed out that his remarks would focus on whether the failure of evidence to support ACP means that the concept itself is fundamentally flawed, its implementation to date has been flawed, or the methods of evaluating how well it works have been flawed.

Halpern explained that 5 years ago, he wrote a commentary in which he claimed there was no strong evidence to endorse nearly any intervention to support end-of-life care (Halpern, 2015). This claim, he recounted, did not sit well with many ACP proponents. Halpern explained that he no longer holds that view, given that the past 5 years have produced high-quality evidence in many domains supportive of serious illness care. He noted that the scoping review that Sudore presented (McMahan et al., 2020) encapsulates the breadth of evidence that researchers have generated in the ACP space.

While the studies were of high quality based on Jadad scoring,[18] noted Halpern, not all of the studies in that review were truly high quality, in that they did not make any statements about the quality of the outcome measures or methods used to evaluate those outcomes. As a result, Halpern questioned whether the overall evidence base was quite as strong as some have portrayed it to be. In fact, he added, there is no consistent evidence that ACP achieves desired outcomes, such as goal-concordant care, quality of life for both patients and family members, or reduced health care use (Ashana et al., 2019; Halpern et al., 2020).

Halpern argued that errors in implementation and/or evaluation may account for weaknesses in the evidence base, and he listed four ways in which implementation and/or evaluation have been flawed, given that the studies:

1. focused on treatments rather than goals and health states;
2. targeted patients too broadly;
3. measured success with the wrong outcomes; and
4. failed to consider other processes, structures, and reimbursement models for supportive care that must be in place to prevent rushing to the hospital in an emergency.

Regarding the focus on treatments, Halpern cited a study that he and his team conducted in which they randomly assigned 200 seriously ill hospitalized patients to make choices about life support treatments, either deliberatively or based intuitively on gut instinct (Rubin et al., 2019). Both

---

[18] Jadad scoring judges the methodological quality of a research study based on randomization, blinding, and dropouts (Jadad et al., 1996).

approaches yielded identical distributions of choices to receive a variety of forms of life support under a variety of clinical circumstances. In fact, the deliberative group may have made worse decisions, said Halpern. "In many scenarios, they more commonly made choices to receive or not receive interventions that would put them into health states that they themselves had deemed equal to or worse than death," said Halpern. "This is a cautionary note for those who think that decision aids are going to be our way forward in improving advance care planning."

In that same study, Halpern noted that he and his colleagues also asked seriously ill patients to identify whether a series of health states were equal to or worse than death (see Figure 4). The results showed that most people indicated various health states they could see themselves developing, such as bowel and bladder incontinence, relying on machines to live, the inability to get out of bed, living in a nursing home, experiencing moderate pain all of the time, or being confused all of the time, that would be similar to or worse than death (Rubin et al., 2019). This work, said Halpern, has motivated him to explore whether states worse than death can be a concept used in greater depth as a potential means of eliciting patient values.

Halpern explained that one of his colleagues has been conducting semi-structured interviews with seriously ill patients and found that nearly all of them can spontaneously identify health states that are worse than death. He said,

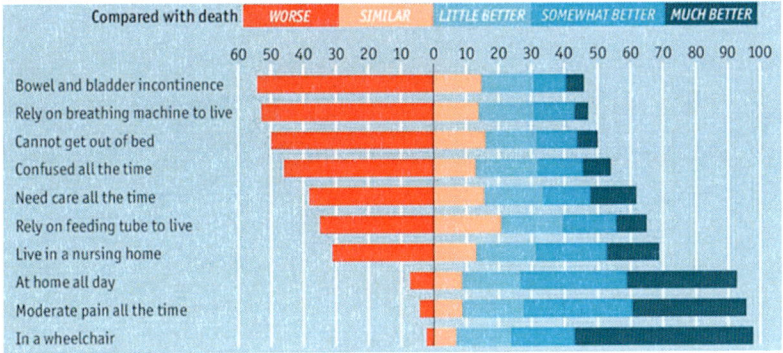

**FIGURE 4** Seriously ill, hospitalized patients rated whether various states of functional disability were better or worse than death.
SOURCES: Scott Halpern presentation, November 2, 2020; *The Economist*, 2016.

The fact that these people can spontaneously identify discrete health states that they would say are equal to or worse than death and, importantly, that they can consistently articulate many reasons for why those health states are worse than death, gives me a great deal of optimism that this might be one path forward in terms of better eliciting underlying goals and values.

Turning to the issue of targeting patients too broadly, Halpern said too many studies have enrolled patients who are either too sick or too well to benefit from ACP; the latter have not yet learned what living with a serious illness is like, so their judgments about what they would want in such a state are not adequately informed. In support of the first of these possibilities, Halpern cited a 2014 systematic review that found a direct relationship between people's level of serious illness and the stability of their end-of-life treatment preferences over time (Auriemma et al., 2014): only 60 percent of older patients without any serious illness had stable preferences over time, while stability improved appreciably for individuals in more progressively ill cohorts.

Another related study is an oft-cited RCT that concluded that ACP improves end-of-life care and patient satisfaction and reduces stress, anxiety, and depression in surviving relatives (Detering et al., 2010). In Halpern's view, this study's weakness was that patients were enrolled so late in their illness that they were not receiving ACP. "The overwhelming majority of patients who were screened for eligibility were excluded because they had either already died or had already lost decisional capacity, really calling into question [the] utility of the intervention in those settings," said Halpern. "There was also limited survival time left for the benefits of the interventions, if any, to have manifested, so this is sort of the other end of the problem of targeting patients."

In Halpern's view, the wrong outcomes are being used to measure ACP success. He noted that panelists in earlier sessions claimed that while goal-concordant care was the ultimate measure (Sudore et al., 2018a), it was not a practical measure for assessing ACP value. However, he pointed out, ongoing research is beginning to show that it is feasible to have blinded raters evaluate the goals of care and then different raters evaluate the care actually received. Early results indicate that goals of care are not often documented, but when they are, goal concordance rates are high, making this a potential method for evaluating ACP, said Halpern.

Halpern concluded his presentation with two points. First, even when perfectly designed and implemented, ACP will not work in a vacuum. Rather, it needs to be implemented in concert with a reimbursement system that incentivizes value-based care to ensure residential monitoring and a backup plan, instead of rushing people to the hospital in an emergency. Second, new approaches are needed to help people articulate their goals and to measure goal concordance.

### Advance Care Planning: Ethical Challenges

Rebecca Dresser, Daniel Noyes Kirby Professor of Law emerita at the Washington University in St. Louis School of Law, noted that her remarks would focus on the complex patient populations that suffer from conditions in which cognitive and physical decline occurs over long periods, such as dementia. She explained the increasing concern that current ACP practices are not suitable for people with dementia, leading to a number of proposals to create dementia-specific directives. She pointed out that Nevada passed a law in 2019[19] formally recognizing a dementia-specific directive, though she thought it was poorly written and confusing.

Dresser noted that there are conflicting interests in creating such directives. She posed the question of whether people should be allowed to discriminate against their "future selves" by empowering them to make medical decisions that conflict with their later interests and concerns as individuals living with dementia. She noted the clash of values between respecting the individual autonomy of people engaging in ACP and expressing their preferences versus protecting people with a disability such as dementia. Dresser identified three reasons to limit such directives:

1. The barriers to informed choice,
2. The deficiencies in the ability to predict quality of life with dementia, and
3. The potential for harm to people living with dementia.

Dresser noted that there are many barriers to informed choice, and in her view, it seems impossible to have sufficient information about risks and benefits to make specific choices, particularly in terms of understanding what the quality of life of a person with dementia will be in the future. Certainly, people with dementia experience problems such as confusion, distress, and anxiety, noted Dresser, but many of them report and exhibit

---

[19] For more information, see https://www.leg.state.nv.us/App/NELIS/REL/80th2019/Bill/6124/Overview (accessed December 10, 2020).

contentment, happiness, and joy much of the time, particularly if they are living in appropriate care settings. In addition, added Dresser, people can lose insight as the condition progresses, becoming less concerned about their losses and adjusting to their changed circumstances. At the same time, public discussion emphasizes the tragedy of dementia, which, Dresser explained, influences the way many people think about ACP and future dementia care.

Dresser then turned to the issue of affective forecasting errors. "Even people who stay well informed about the variety of experiences people with dementia have can make inaccurate predictions about how they are going to feel if they get dementia," explained Dresser. She also noted the general tendency for people to overestimate the negative effects of illness on subjective well-being (Charles and Gafni, 2006; Halpern and Arnold, 2008) and that people living with a wide range of disabilities are happier and enjoy a higher quality of life than people without disabilities think they are. Bioethicists, said Dresser, have started writing about the concept of transformative experience to explain a healthy person's inability to make good choices about future care. Dresser stressed that transformative experiences, such as becoming a parent or developing dementia, can change perceptions and preferences in ways the person cannot imagine ahead of time. Competent individuals have the power to revise treatment preferences as they deal with new health situations. Yet, giving absolute authority to ACP denies incompetent patients the same access to treatment that fits their contemporaneous situations, explained Dresser.

In many cases, individuals with decisional incapacity still have health care views and preferences and the ability to participate in health choices, although they may need help, said Dresser. She added that the legal and ethical concepts of assent and dissent recognize this, and the emerging practice of supported decision making allows people with cognitive impairments to collaborate with a trusted partner in deciding about the health care they receive.

Dresser concluded with three suggestions to improve ACP for people with dementia:

1. Promote a better understanding of the potential futures for those with serious illness.
2. Recognize how stigma can shape individual preferences, professional judgments, and community attitudes.
3. Develop approaches to ACP that recognize the interests and concerns of people with dementia and other intellectual disabilities.

## Advancing the Language of Advance Care Planning: A Messaging Research Project

Anna Gosline, senior director of strategic initiatives, Blue Cross Blue Shield of Massachusetts and executive director of the Massachusetts Coalition for Serious Illness Care, focused her remarks on the results of a public opinion project her organization conducted in 2019 that highlighted the opportunity to find new approaches for engaging the community in ACP. She noted that her organization has started a second, similar study focused on communities of color, people with disabilities, and other at-risk populations. "Not everyone experiences the language and approaches common to advance care planning similarly, and we think those differences are likely to have [been] magnified during this time of COVID," said Gosline.

Gosline explained that the project started in 2016 with a baseline survey asking questions about ACP and experiences with the death of a loved one, followed by an open-ended, follow-up survey in 2017 and a tracking survey in 2018 that included comparisons to the results of a large national survey conducted by the Kaiser Family Foundation. Gosline shared four main findings from this work:

1. The public strongly equates ACP with death, do-not-resuscitate orders, and life-sustaining treatment choices.
2. Despite significant attention, energy, and activity in Massachusetts, the state is similar to the rest of the nation with respect to levels of ACP engagement, though bereaved caregivers' assessments of their loved one's care improved.
3. There are significant disparities in ACP engagement and inequities in experiences at the end of life across race, ethnicity, income, and education.
4. Changes in outcomes and experiences of care at the end of life can improve even without population-level changes in traditional ACP activities.

These findings prompted Gosline and her colleagues to ask themselves how they might approach ACP differently from a public communications perspective. The result was messaging designed to purposefully shift the language away from end-of-life care, life-sustaining treatment choices, and documentation and instead emphasize the process and conversations. "Our hope was that by using methodologically rigorous research, we could reveal new approaches that would work across the population as a whole but also speak to the people who are not already engaging in advance care planning," Gosline explained.

Gosline noted that, in the first phase of this project, she and her colleagues developed a nationally representative, quantitative survey asking questions about ACP behaviors and other variables that expert advisors and the literature suggested were connected to ACP completion, such as personality traits, health status, and religion. The team then used cluster analysis to create a set of five meaningful segments representing people's attitudes and experiences, which are the most important foundations for testing messages, concepts, and language. The segments were categorized as worried action takers, self-assured action takers, disengaged worriers, confident independents, and self-reliant skeptics.

Action takers, Gosline explained, had completed a document naming a surrogate and listing their wishes for care, while non-action takers did not. In all other ways, the five segments were different. For example, worried action takers (10 percent of the sample) completed ACP documents because they were worried about not getting enough life-extending care, driven by a very high percentage of them having recently experienced making decisions on behalf of an incapacitated loved one. The self-assured action takers (24 percent of the sample), on the other hand, likely completed ACP documents because of cultural expectations and were not worried about a future serious illness.

The non-action takers, Gosline explained, were also unique in their own way. For example, the disengaged worriers, who had the lowest income, were most diverse, had the lowest education level, and were the largest segment of the sample (34 percent), picked every possible reason why they had not engaged in ACP. Confident independents (18 percent), on the other hand, did not think they needed ACP, commenting that their spouses would know what to do. The self-reliant skeptics (14 percent) were characterized by their marked distrust of the health care system. Gosline noted that though her team did not build these segments based on demographics, the segments clearly had demographic commonalities. Self-assured action takers, for instance, were disproportionately retired Americans, while worried action takers and disengaged worriers were disproportionately Black Americans. She also pointed out that these segments provide the foundation for ensuring that when her team is testing ideas about understanding and language, they do so in a way that reveals diverse opinions and experiences.

Gosline shared that she and her colleagues then tested five messages supporting ACP (see Table 1) on a nationally representative sample of 150

**TABLE 1** Five Messages Supporting Advance Care Planning

| Category | Example Message |
|---|---|
| **Love/Gift**<br>Love means speaking up. | If any of us became seriously ill, those closest to us may have to make important decisions about our care. Asking and sharing what would matter most to each other in that event is an act of love and kindness that can make future decisions easier—a gift we can give to those who matter most. |
| **Peace of mind**<br>There's no need to wonder. | The future is full of unknowns, but open conversations can pave the way to clarity, no matter what happens with our health. Having conversations about serious illness and the kind of care that's right for us gives us a shared understanding that fosters peace of mind. |
| **Demand the right care**<br>We can have a say in our care. | Getting the health care we need often involves decisions, and we can and should speak up about the kind of care that works for us and ask doctors to understand what matters to us. Asking for what we want from our care also means telling those closest to us what we'd want if we couldn't make decisions for ourselves. |
| **Control (via a decision maker)**<br>Conversations clarify. | We can't plan for everything, but we can help manage life's unknowns by talking openly about what matters to us and what we'd want most if we became seriously ill. Conversations about things we can't control can actually help to give us a sense of control. |
| **Honor loved ones' wishes**<br>Caring means learning what matters to them. | There may be a time when we have to help the people closest to us—our friends, our spouses, our parents or grandparents—get the care that's right for them. Delivering on that promise means understanding what is most important to them in the face of serious illness. |

SOURCES: Anna Gosline presentation, November 2, 2020; Massachusetts Coalition for Serious Illness Care, 2019.

people, asking them to highlight language that did or did not resonate with them and note any that was off-putting. Some messages worked well, and some did not. The concept of peace of mind did not resonate broadly across all five segments, especially for lower-income households that thought it might be exclusionary, given the possible expenses of guaranteeing someone peace of mind at the end of life. Similarly, added Gosline, the concept of lessening or easing the burden on caregivers was viewed negatively, with some individuals feeling it should not be a burden to care for a loved one, while others thought that having the conversation does not really ease the burden of having loved ones who are seriously ill. Comparing ACP to wellness and an annual check-up was also viewed as negative and largely implausible.

Gosline shared that most people preferred the messages about controlling their care and demanding the right care, which she explained are not mutually exclusive and point to different conceptual elements among the processes that ACP comprises. Control, or conversations to clarify, emphasizes selecting a surrogate decision maker in the case of unexpected incapacity, while demanding the right care emphasized expectations and demands for shared decision making by the patient as part of the clinical process. Gosline noted that it became clear as testing proceeded that language or phrases such as "values, goals, and preferences" have become another euphemism for dying, which may be because the only time clinicians start talking about values, goals, and preferences is when curative treatments have failed.

In closing, Gosline said there were two take-home messages that might provide a new way to move ACP upstream for all. First, everyone needs a health proxy, but unexpected incapacity is unlikely for younger and healthier groups, so they may logically put other life priorities first. In her opinion, this supports keeping messages light and making the ACP process as easy as possible. Second, perhaps the best way to prepare people for serious illness decisions is a lifelong experience with and expectation of shared decision making with trusted health care clinicians in health care systems. Additionally, health care clinicians and systems need to focus on cultural humility, respect, aligning care with priorities, and identifying and addressing bias and structural racism, said Gosline. This approach requires being intentional about listening to an individual's life priorities and preferences and talking about treatment benefits, costs, and trade-offs. "This way, we are starting early in helping people understand how to translate their lives and experiences into medical decisions, and that way, we are never waiting for that final and clear moment when death is on the horizon to talk about goals," concluded Gosline.

## Discussion

Session moderator Kimberly Johnson, associate professor of medicine at the Duke University School of Medicine, opened the discussion by noting that the speakers addressed ACP at different points along the continuum—from community-based messaging to early ACP within the context of a specific chronic illness to the end of life. She asked the panelists how ACP researchers should be thinking differently about the outcomes they are evaluating. Halpern replied that the approach to ACP may be a separate issue from the right way to evaluate outcomes. In his view, the evaluation framework stems from what the general goals are, and the goals of ACP have been clear for some time. Less clear, he said, has been the approach to ACP, its benefits, and its ability to achieve those goals. Halpern said,

> We operate in a health care system where the default [leans] strongly toward providing intensive and resuscitative care unless or until someone says stop—so the entire advent of advance care planning is arguably most pertinent to those who would like to set some limitations. But I think the concept of goal-concordant care recognizes that potentially there are virtues to thinking in advance that go in both directions, conceivably toward more or less aggressive care, and tailoring the care received to the goals of the individual seems unambiguous and something we ought to be striving for.

Gosline noted that her team learned from their work on messaging that people want high-quality care and understand that ACP should be part of the entire clinical interaction. In terms of measurement, the results of her work suggest that people want measures to reflect whether they feel they are in control, listened to, and supported in their decision making.

Dresser said the crux of the moral problem with ACP in terms of individuals with dementia or other intellectual impairments is that ACP could deprive affected people of the ability to make decisions that reflect their contemporaneous circumstances. However, conditions such as dementia or other intellectual impairments do not mean the individual cannot participate in decision making. In fact, she said, empirical research shows that when surrogates are working with people with dementia, they tend to see it primarily as a collaborative approach where they are interacting and reaching a common decision. Dresser pointed out that a number of states have recognized the concept of supported decision making that allows people with intellectual impairment to choose a trusted person to make decisions collaboratively. "What we need to do is recognize that advance care planning should be discussed with people and conceptually thought about as something that involves not just the planner but the individual as he or she evolves or changes and that that individual needs to be part of the consideration, too," said Dresser. "We have neglected the so-called 'best interest standard,' and that is where we need to get better in order to balance these two ethical considerations of well-being for the person with the disability and respect for autonomy."

Johnson's final question focused on approaches to ACP that may incorporate the broader context in which people are making these decisions, including their social determinants, their cultural beliefs, and other social constructs. Gosline replied that there are emerging sets of conversational constructs and frameworks, such as the What Matters toolkit from Patient Priorities Care,[20] that pull in the broader context to help people understand how their life experiences, goals, and preferences on an ongoing basis should be feeding into the way they make medical decisions.

## PRACTICAL STEPS TO MORE EFFECTIVE ADVANCE CARE PLANNING

### The Importance of Patients' and Families' Nonmedical Concerns

Rebecca Kirch, executive vice president of policy and programs at NPAF, began the workshop's penultimate panel by explaining that her organization represents people with more than 600 different diagnoses and largely focuses on supporting the needs of the working poor. She spoke about what she called the "untold backstory" of the things that are on families' and patients' minds when they are confronting serious illness: insurance coverage, financial impairments that accompany the physical impairments resulting from illness, and household material hardships that are added on top of the diagnosis and the experience with making decisions about treatment.

Kirch explained that her organization uses community-based discussion sessions to build confidence in people to talk about what is on their minds in the context of health care. Feedback from these sessions (known as Can We Talk?[21]) identified four main concerns—the overall financial cost of treatment, the possibility of dying, and the short- and long-term side effects of treatment—none of which appear on an advance directive. NPAF patients ranked avoiding financial distress as their most important goal of care, with being able to take care of themselves and their families second. Kirch explained that financial and social needs are not an afterthought, yet these are often overlooked elements of ACP conversations. "In the context

---

[20] For more information, see https://patientprioritiescare.org (accessed December 17, 2020).

[21] For more information, see https://www.npaf.org/can-we-talk (accessed December 10, 2020).

of advance care planning that focuses on advance directives, we are missing the mark if we only focus on that space," said Kirch.

Kirch emphasized the importance of expanding ACP to go beyond the health care system and take advantage of the resources that are available in order to address community-based needs. Doing so, said Kirch, will help with clinical outcomes as well as peace of mind and adherence to treatment recommendations.

Kirch then recounted her own family's experience with ACP, first when she lost her brother to lung cancer a decade ago and then when her mother was diagnosed with amyotrophic lateral sclerosis. Kirch and her family knew they had to develop plans for palliative care and make sure everything they arranged would fit with her mother's goals, which were influenced by her mother's sister's experience with polio when her mother and aunt were young. Kirch shared that at the time of her diagnosis, her mother's concerns were about quality of life and living and avoiding any type of artificial breathing, and she knew exactly what she did and did not want. Kirch recounted that her mother wanted to know what it was going to be like when she lost the ability to breathe on her own. Kirch set up a palliative care visit to walk her mom through what that would be like and what support would be available.

In contrast, Kirch explained, when her stepmother was diagnosed with colon cancer and Kirch arranged for a palliative care visit, the palliative care provider only focused on completing the advance directive, which was not what the family needed at the time. Rather, Kirch pointed out, it was what the health system wanted. "We need to think about how can we fix that disconnect by focusing on what patients and families need in the moment, and then we can get to what the health system needs through a process of building trust," said Kirch.

In closing, Kirch pointed out that the bottom line is the need to move beyond conditioning everyone to talk only about their medical conditions and instead support the need for relatable information so that people can make good choices based on what they consider to be their top needs and concerns, which is very different from what medical professionals need. She also highlighted the idea that empathic communication skills and trust must be built between patients and health professionals through training and practice. From a policy perspective, she noted that caregiving is a major cost-sharing and quality care delivery contribution that should be explicitly valued and supported. Finally, quality measures and payment should formalize accountability for person-centered communication skills training and practice that identifies patients' priorities and meets their needs.

### Implementing Advance Care Planning in the Hospital Setting

Julie Childers, associate professor of medicine in the Division of General Internal Medicine at the University of Pittsburgh, opened her remarks with a description of a scenario common to most hospital-based clinicians; an elderly person with advanced disease and comorbidities comes to the ED in cardiac arrest or experiencing another kind of crisis and is resuscitated. Later, when the family arrives, clinicians are told that the patient would not have wanted these interventions. Childers explained that the patient often had a POLST form from a previous admission, had written an advance directive, or had otherwise made their wishes known, but the ED clinicians had no access to these documented decisions. Childers stressed that the lesson is that ACP done in the past does not have much meaning without the ability to communicate it to present and future situations.

Childers explained that carrying out an advance care plan has two parts. First, hospital clinicians have to be able to access previous patient discussions. Second, those discussions need to be implemented, which requires communicating with patients or families about them and how to implement them in the current setting. At the University of Pittsburgh Medical Center, Childers explained, the solution to the first part involved changing the organization's EHR so that an advance directive that has been scanned into the system is displayed prominently on the top bar of each EHR record. In addition, any time a clinician has a code status discussion with a patient, they are required to describe in an accompanying text box precisely what they discussed. Childers added that the EHR also has a dedicated and searchable goals-of-care template that enables a clinician to track every previous discussion with a patient in the health system.

Showing examples of the EHR's summary page, CPR status page, and the area where a clinician can enter goals of care or ACP conversations, Childers explained that these EHRs were designed to make it easy for clinicians to see what happened in the past and easily document subsequent conversations with the patient. Having this information, she explained, allows her to tailor a current conversation to identify any changes in the patient's perception of their condition when they were in a clinical situation they had not envisioned when they previously voiced their wishes and preferences. This information also allows the clinician to avoid repeating conversations.

"A patient with advanced illness who is accepting life-sustaining treatment at the current time often gets asked the same question and is forced into the same discussion over and over again, and then the patient eventually feels a lack of trust in the health care system and feels like their wishes and decisions are not respected," explained Childers. Having a repeat conversation when a patient is in crisis can also place a heavy decision-making burden on them at a time when they may be emotional about how they are feeling physically, she added.

Childers and her colleagues have developed a framework that calls for first evaluating the evidence that previous decisions still apply (Childers et al., 2021). This entails determining how recent the decision was, how many times the patient made the same decision, how much information is available about the values that led to the decision, and how similar the previous clinical scenario is to the one now facing the patient. If there is strong evidence that the previous decision still applies, the values were laid out clearly, and the decision is fairly recent, the clinician just needs to do a quick check-in that simply asks the patient if they remember what they decided and if anything has changed, said Childers. If the answer is no, the clinician proposes a clinical plan that fits the decision. Childers pointed out that this takes the burden of making another decision off of the patient. If the evidence is weaker, the clinician will ask the patient to talk about what they were thinking at the time they made the decision to make sure the reasoning and values are consistent with what their advance directive says.

In Childers's view, the best way to implement advance care plans is to make it easy to find ACP documentation in the EHR, document the values and reasons behind decision making in discussions about goals of care, and carry previous decisions forward intelligently. The latter, said Childers, should include evaluating the evidence, talking to the patient, and using that discussion to carry forward the previous decision—unless there is sufficient justification for why the previous decision should be changed.

### The Health System Perspective on Practical Steps to More Effective Advance Care Planning

Nina Ross O'Connor, chief of palliative care at Penn Medicine, presented an approach to building a system to create effective ACP at the health system level. In thinking about this problem, she and her colleagues considered each of the layers in the safety net that ensures that every patient has a conversation about what really matters to them.

There are three important questions to ask from the health system perspective when it comes to thinking about how to implement ACP:

1. Which patients and clinicians should the system focus on?
2. What outcome is the system trying to drive (i.e., is it a conversation or a document)?
3. How can we ensure that the process is consistent and of high quality?

The first question is the hardest to address, said O'Connor. While there are compelling reasons to target every patient for ACP, a health system wants to first prioritize those who are seriously ill or frail. This leads to a process of prioritizing practices and service lines with a high proportion of seriously ill patients, such as the cancer service line; heart and vascular service line; geriatrics, including long-term care clinicians; and primary care, with a focus on the system's longitudinal care management program. This is not to say that other patients cannot be engaged in ACP, she noted, but being deliberate about targeting certain groups is helpful.

The next step, said O'Connor, is to focus on patients who might benefit most, including those who ask for ACP in advance. There are, however, others who will never bring up ACP unless they are asked about it by someone they trust. O'Connor shared that one strategy her institution uses is to ask the "surprise question": Would you be surprised if this patient died in the next 2 years? She noted evidence that this is actually effective at identifying patients who would benefit from ACP (Lakin et al., 2019). In addition, O'Connor and her colleagues are starting to use data and predictive analytics to ensure that they do not miss anyone with serious illness. This initiative, which is operating in cancer care, is called Conversation Connect, and it uses a machine learning algorithm to mine data in the system's EHR to identify patients who might be at increased risk of mortality and do not have a documented conversation in their EHR (Manz et al., 2020). She noted that it notifies their clinician with a text on the day they are coming in for an appointment that asks them to consider having a serious illness conversation. The system also provides clinicians with feedback in terms of whether all of their patients were at least offered the opportunity to have a conversation.

O'Connor explained that when determining which clinicians to target, it is important to consider how to build a scalable workforce for ACP that does not rely solely on palliative care specialists. O'Connor noted that her health care system is training palliative care champions in various treatment areas, who receive additional training on ACP and can serve as resources for patients and peers. Eventually, the system will consider how to train all of its clinicians in palliative care skills.

The goal at Penn Medicine is to highlight conversations, said O'Connor, whereas the documents are the product of some of those conversations, which are captured in a consistent and easy-to-retrieve location in the EHR. O'Connor pointed out that the system's goal is that 100 percent of patients with a serious illness will have a documented conversation about their goals, values, and priorities. O'Connor clarified that this is not always a medical conversation, and it could include any number of nonmedical priorities, such as financial and social concerns. Focusing on conversations unifies the system around one common goal that can be measured and shared with each clinician, which drives improvements in education and interventions. "That decision to focus on conversations leads to metrics that allow us to monitor and keep improving our performance and make sure that all the patients have conversations," said O'Connor.

Once a health system decides which patients will be its initial target group and what outcome it will target, it has an ethical obligation to make sure that those conversations are of high quality, that it is a safe experience for patients to talk about these things, and that what patients and families experience is consistent across the system, said O'Connor. With many ways to do this, O'Connor's system partnered with Ariadne Labs[22] to use the serious illness conversation guide. She added that this guide uses patient-tested language and mostly open-ended questions that help clinicians start conversations, ensure that those conversations focus on what really matters to patients, and avoid making the conversations overly medical. Training clinicians is also important, and O'Connor noted that Penn Medicine created a 3-hour training that includes follow-up coaching. She stated that training will not produce change unless there is system change too. For O'Connor and her colleagues, that involved thinking about how they prepare patients, document conversations, and remind clinicians about the importance of having these conversations. "You put that all together to try to achieve quality and consistency," said O'Connor.

The next step is to set up a system to monitor the program's performance and identify any areas that need to be adjusted to improve.

---

[22] For more information, see https://www.ariadnelabs.org (accessed December 10, 2020).

O'Connor explained that the system monitors performance in two ways: tracking conversations and getting periodic patient feedback.

In closing, O'Connor reiterated several key take-home lessons for health systems:

- Define target populations; patients with serious illness and frailty should be top priority.
- Use data science to identify patients to prioritize for ACP.
- Conversations are the goal; some conversations (but not all) result in an advance directive.
- Recognize that scalable training is critical to ensure consistent, high-quality ACP conversations.
- Track and monitor conversations for ongoing program evaluation.

**Discussion**

Hillary Lum, associate professor of medicine-geriatrics at the University of Colorado School of Medicine and moderator of the discussion session, asked the panelists how they ensure that high-quality conversations between clinicians and patients are less medical and more about values and preferences. Childers replied that her institution's system-wide training program works with clinicians, residents, and fellows to teach them how to speak in "regular English," which includes asking open-ended questions that focus on identifying someone's biggest priorities and what is important to them going forward. Clinicians then decide on both a medical plan and a social plan, to which her system has access, which together can satisfy a patient's medical, personal, and social needs.

Kirch noted that patients and families come to a medical appointment conditioned to talk only about their health, which means that they need help gaining the confidence to talk about themselves as people with human needs and not just as a person with a disease. People feel comfortable talking about what is important to them in the context of their life flow, not what is important in terms of the health system's clinical flow. However, ACP often medicalizes people's conditions so "when we try to make those two things fit, there is nothing but dissonance and a lack of receptivity," said Kirch. "The opportunity is to restore that faith and trust in patients who have expertise in their lived experience and help guide the care planning conversations that happen."

O'Connor added that while it may not seem that way to patients and their families, clinicians do get quite nervous and anxious about having these conversations, which can cause them to retreat into clinical language. Training, as Childers said, is a good way to lower that anxiety. O'Connor also pointed out that clinicians have found that conversation anchors or guides can help them keep their comments open ended.[23] In terms of who to train, O'Connor said that depends on the practice and patient population. For example, in her institution's cancer service line, patients want to have these conversations specifically with their oncologist, so training has focused on the oncologists, as well as advance practice providers and social workers. In primary care, where care is team based, community health workers, nurse navigators, and care managers receive training. The key, said O'Connor, is to train the people that the patient trusts and to recognize that what does not work is to insert someone who is not the primary clinician for the patient's condition.

O'Connor remarked that one difficult part of training is getting clinicians over the initial hurdle of having these conversations and feeling confident in their ability to do so. Once they gain confidence, they find that having the conversations makes their work more meaningful, and that reinforces this work. In addition, said O'Connor, it is important that clinicians receive feedback, particularly from patients.

Childers seconded that approach and emphasized that conducting trainings and having these conversations help reinforce the culture. She commented that getting to clinicians early in their training as medical professionals can help them see this as a normal part of medical care. Having trainees do a palliative care rotation can help, too, said Childers. Kirch reiterated that incentivizing training as an accountability measure could also reinforce the importance of having these conversations. She added that she would like to see every clinician participate in the VitalTalk program[24] before they start seeing patients.

---

[23] Various organizations produce such guides, including the Institute for Human Caring (http://www.instituteforhumancaring.org/documents/Providers/SI-Clinician-Reference-Guide.pdf), CoMagine Health (https://healthinsight.org/tools-and-resources/send/50-in-person-events/298-eol-using-the-serious-illness-conversation-guide), Ariadne Labs (https://www.ariadnelabs.org/areas-of-work/serious-illness-care/resources/#Downloads&%20Tools), and the Institute for Healthcare Improvement (http://www.ihi.org/_layouts/15/ihi/login/login.aspx?ReturnURL=%2fresources%2fPages%2fTools%2fConversation-Ready-Toolkit-for-Clinicians.aspx), among others (all websites accessed December 17, 2020).

[24] Additional information is available at https://www.vitaltalk.org (accessed February 16, 2021).

Lum then asked the panelists if they have examples of how their institutions have leveraged a value-based payment program to help fuel this work. O'Connor said her organization has taught its physicians about ACP billing codes, which is how they are reimbursed for these conversations, but the effects have been mixed. While physicians have found the codes valuable, O'Connor explained, they can result in charging the patient an extra copay, which can be a barrier. In addition, the codes are complicated to use and require extra documentation. Overall, O'Connor views the availability of ACP billing codes as a step forward. O'Connor pointed out that some of her institution's practices are participating in the Oncology Care model[25] or other alternative payment models, such as Primary Care First,[26] that use quality metrics that reward having ACP conversations. Childers cautioned that there is a tension between desiring clinicians to want to do things because it is the right thing versus because they will get paid for it. She noted that the danger in having various incentives is that it might enable people to complete the minimum requirements rather than truly caring about and investing in the conversations.

Lum noted the difficulty in measuring the quality of conversations and asked if the panelists used strategies beyond getting patient testimonials. O'Connor said her institution uses a common documentation template that includes discussion of prognosis and specific care treatment decisions, as well as places to document things such as what gives a particular patient strength and what the patient's greatest worries and priorities are. Her organization reviews the EHR to see to what extent the clinician has completed those domains, how many conversations have more than just CPR status, and how many include a prognostic discussion. In addition, her organization talks to clinicians who use the conversations to find out if they help the clinicians take better care of their patients.

Childers said that making changes in the EHR and incentivizing clinicians to use the goals-of-care template in the EHR was a first step for her organization. The second step, currently ongoing, is to examine what the clinicians have documented in the template and assess how much of it reflects the elements of a good discussion. She noted that while she is not directly involved in that effort, she has received e-mail feedback about her own use of the template.

---

[25] Additional information is available at https://innovation.cms.gov/innovation-models/oncology-care (accessed February 16, 2021).

[26] Additional information is available at https://innovation.cms.gov/innovation-models/primary-care-first-model-options (accessed February 16, 2021).

## PANEL DISCUSSION

The workshop's final session consisted of four panelists reflecting on what they had heard over the 2 days of the workshop: Reverend Cynthia Carter Perrilliat, executive director of the Alameda County Care Alliance; Diane Meier, director of the Center to Advance Palliative Care; Mildred Solomon, president of The Hastings Center; and Abraham Brody, associate professor of nursing and medicine and associate director of the Hartford Institute for Geriatric Nursing at the New York University Rory Meyers College of Nursing. Arnold moderated the session and opened the discussion by asking the four panelists to list their key take-home messages from all of the presentations in the virtual workshop.

Perrilliat noted that first and foremost, it is clear that ACP conversations are tremendously complex and very human, something that is often overlooked by clinicians coming from a medical and scientific perspective. She noted that Stuart's and Harris's personal stories pointed out the complexity of gathering information and that systems often do not communicate with one another. Finally, Perrilliat noted that while 30 years of research has been devoted to ACP, more work is needed to apply the lessons highlighted at the workshop to make the ACP process truly person centered.

Meier said the discussions reminded her of learning about Maslow's hierarchy of needs,[27] which cites access to food, water, and shelter as the most important human needs. Kirch's data, however, show that many families are not confident about being able to satisfy those needs and are rightfully worried that a serious medical illness will bankrupt them or that no one can take care of them at home and their only option, in a crisis, is to call 911. "It feels to me as if those of us working to advance ACP are often in our little corner focused on maximizing patient self-determination and autonomy, and the reality is over here on the other side of the room," said Meier. "Our faith in this illusion of control about what happens to people with serious illness causes us to focus on things that are really not at the top of the priority list for actual patients and families."

Meier emphasized that for patients and families, priority items are avoiding bankruptcy, paying for their children's education, putting food on

---

[27] Maslow's hierarchy of needs is a motivational theory in psychology comprising a five-tier model of human needs, often depicted as hierarchical levels within a pyramid (McLeod, 2020).

the table, and getting help if they are caring for a seriously ill loved one, yet the health care system does not enable any of that, and neither does society. Meier shared that she was reminded of the joke about someone dropping their keys in the parking lot and looking for them under the streetlight because the light is better there. "The patient's problems are in the dark parking lot, and we are trying to address their problems under the streetlight that is advance care planning," she said. Her final thought was that health care professionals have a larger humanistic vision, and the field needs to embrace that vision and push for a reallocation of health care resources to meet actual human needs. In other words, ACP should not be a priority until the larger societal problems regarding health care are solved.

Agreeing with most of Meier's comments, Solomon said she was excited about the systems-oriented approaches to ensure that ACP conversations of the right type occur with the right sets of patients that several of the speakers addressed. She noted, too, the importance of training providers to be brave enough to be honest with patients and families about what the future holds for them as part of the ACP conversation.

Solomon also said she shared the frustration that ACP research has been ongoing for 30 years and the tools and talents are still mainly medical, while the problems to solve are mainly social, financial, and political. Unlike Meier, she does not think the takeaway is to stop doing ACP until the bigger social, political, and financial problems are solved. "I think we have to do both," said Solomon. For her, though, the larger issue about the societal and political will to provide the support that an aging population requires is a "citizenship question," which is why she believes doing both is the right approach. Solomon explained,

> We can enhance advance care planning in systemic ways if we get smarter and more organizationally oriented, but I think that since health care professionals are highly esteemed, since they know these issues more than anybody else, there is a citizenship role that we can all play as well to try to put in place the kind of society that we want to be, not just the kind of health care system we want to be.

Brody commented on opportunities to focus on the advocacy needed to shift from a medical environment and put more resources into social programs. Brody pointed to the 120 academic medical centers that account for 25 percent of U.S. health care spending while only treating about 5 percent of the population. He shared that when he sits down for ACP or goals-of-care conversations and asks patients to tell him about themselves, they almost always start with their medical problems. When he asks them about their lives beyond their medical problems, they look shocked because they are not accustomed to being treated as people instead of patients. He noted that work from the University of Colorado School of Medicine, for example, focused on using community health workers as patient navigators to address ACP, particularly in Latinx populations, and that other programs have social workers take the lead in ACP to shift the conversations out of the medicalized realm.

Perrilliat agreed about the need to look at ACP from a holistic perspective that operates both within and outside the medical system and to involve not just the health care system but the broader community as well. "I think there has to be this congruent approach to really address and attack the needs of [the] community," she said. Turning to the issue of disparities in the health care system raised by some of the workshop participants, Perrilliat explained that the model her organization uses is to provide faith-based community care navigators with extensive training in both ACP and the social determinants of health and social needs. This training also focuses on helping individuals and their caregivers prepare for a doctor's visit and develop a list of important questions they might have so that they make best use of their appointment.

Arnold then asked the panelists to state what they think the health care system should change and what it should stop doing. Meier replied that the first thing to stop doing is conflating ACP with cost savings. Many entities, particularly payers and the government, have been persuaded somehow that ACP is the key to reducing spending. "There are no data to support that, and it worries me to have entities with financial goals leading the charge for better advance care planning," said Meier. "Stop putting forward what we do as a way to reduce health care spending." She added that linking ACP to lower spending only reinforces the public's belief that those who focus on ACP are advocating for interests other than the patient's. In fact, she pointed out, recent research shows that ACP had no impact on health care use (Ashana et al., 2019).

Brody said the health care system must stop traumatizing caregivers and the people they care for, citing research showing that caregivers who have had to go through these complex decision-making processes, all the way from ACP to more immediate goals-of-care conversations, can experience symptoms of PTSD. Part of the reason for that, he said, is because the system pressures people to make these decisions right away. "We traumatize them into trying to make these bivariate decisions that do not need to exist and are not important to them," said Brody, "versus the real issues around who is this person, what was important to them as a person, and how they would want to live." The solution, he said, is changing the focus from clinicians and what they will be forced to do because of indecision and making the process about the patient and caregivers and what is positive about the decisions they are making.

For Solomon, the one thing to stop doing is "worshiping autonomy" and the whole focus on individualism. "I think we should be focusing on beneficence,[28] care, justice, and accountability of the clinical staff," she said. In Solomon's view, there should be a shift from an autonomy-focused process to a systems-oriented process that clearly delineates the responsibilities, obligations, and accountability of the health care system so that it can provide more than the current default pathway into fragmented specialty care. She encouraged systems to designate staff members who will be responsible for holding goals of care conversations, create ways to identify which patients need those conversations, ensure multi-disciplinary participation, and track that they have occurred for the right people at the right time.

Perrilliat, referring to and embracing the aphorism "insanity is doing the same thing over and over again and expecting different results," said it is clear that a different approach is needed to ACP and end-of-life conversations. She suggested developing what she referred to as a "multi-tiered marketing strategy," one that has a layered, congruent effort that occurs in health systems, in communities, and on a national basis and includes language and messaging that speaks to the masses. Perrilliat said,

> There needs to be a reallocation of funds that really embraces this as an important human-centric initiative that is going to impact every single one of us, whether we are in health care, whether we are in hospice, palliative care, you name it. We are all human beings who are going to have to deal with the issues of making decisions about what we want or do not want as we approach life's end, and it has to be an approach that speaks to not just serious illness and the end of life but empowering people to know that what they want for themselves counts.

Arnold, citing the current fascination with personalized medicine, asked Solomon how to make the changes that Meier, Perrilliat, and Brody called for in a society that seems to want timely and personalized care yet is interested in every scientific advance. Solomon said that is the "$64,000 question," and it raises the issue of the powerful hold the technological

---

[28] In health care, "beneficence" means that all medical practitioners have a moral duty to promote the course of action that they believe is in the best interests of the patient.

imperative has on the public's imagination. She said that she takes a long view and believes that health care is on the cusp of doing better in terms of describing what the future holds for individuals with serious illness. She does not believe that it is inconsistent with personalized medicine, just a different matter. What she would like to see is a shift toward more accountability and fulfilling the obligation that clinical teams have to use kind but clear language when they talk to their patients so that patients better understand the reality of their circumstances.

Meier reminded everyone that ethical principles beyond autonomy and self-determination underlie the practice of health care, including justice and equity, beneficence, doing good for patients, doing good in a way that aligns with what the patient thinks is good, and not doing harm to patients. "All our focus is on honoring self-determination, and we have let the other ethical principles atrophy in terms of their day-to-day influence on our practice. I think it has deformed the practice of medicine as we essentially ignore these huge social factors that determine the outcomes of more than 80 percent of our patients," said Meier.

Meier shared that she strongly believes that

> supporting clinicians to have meaningful conversations with people living with serious illness and their families is valuable because the relationship is valuable, because the relationship creates trust, because the relationship helps the person and their family feel valued as fellow human beings.... I think much of the data that shows positive outcomes supports that belief and that we should invest in it, not because it is going to save us money, but because it invests in the all-important human connection without which no medical care can be of high quality or achieve valuable outcomes.

Solomon responded to Meier by saying it is easy to criticize medicine and health care, but she also believes bioethics deserves some criticism as well. Using her organization as an example, Solomon said she and her colleagues are proud that they published guidelines in the late 1980s on the use of life-sustaining technologies that helped to create the norms for withdrawing or withholding life-sustaining treatments in order to guide bedside decision making. To Meier's point, however, Solomon explained that she and a colleague wrote an essay in 2018 calling on the field of bioethics to do what Meier is asking of medicine; namely to take within its purview not only clinical bedside decision making but also focus on what a just society needs to do to fulfill its duties and obligations to all of its citizens so they can age decently with housing, food availability, and social supports (Berlinger and Solomon, 2018).

As a last question, Arnold asked Perrilliat to what degree this is health care's role versus society's role and asked about a cost for locating it within health care. She replied that there is an obvious cost to do this right and that health care has an important role. However, she believes that more diligence is needed when it comes to the policy level and making policy changes that speak to the notion of justice, equity, and inclusion, and that makes this a societal issue. "Health care is a leader, and we need health care to lead," said Perrilliat, "but we also need to effect this from a policy perspective as well, and I think we would be remiss if we did not include, discuss, communicate, and engage with our political realm in this important subject matter."

## CLOSING REMARKS

Reflecting on the last panel discussion, Arnold remarked that it was important to note how a conversation about ACP led to the consideration of the social determinants of health and policy. He thanked the workshop speakers, participants, and staff for their contributions to the broader discussion and closed the workshop.

## REFERENCES

Ashana, D. C., X. Chen, A. Agiro, G. Sridhar, A. Nguyen, J. Barron, K. Haynes, M. Fisch, D. Debono, S. D. Halpern, and M. O. Harhay. 2019. Advance care planning claims and health care utilization among seriously ill patients near the end of life. *JAMA Network Open* 2(11):e1914471.

Auriemma, C. L., C. A. Nguyen, R. Bronheim, S. Kent, S. Nadiger, D. Pardo, and S. D. Halpern. 2014. Stability of end-of-life preferences: A systematic review of the evidence. *JAMA Internal Medicine* 174(7):1085–1092.

Berlinger, N., and M. Z. Solomon. 2018. Becoming good citizens of aging societies. *Hastings Center Report* 48(S3):S2–S9.

Bischoff, K. E., R. Sudore, Y. Miao, W. J. Boscardin, and A. K. Smith. 2013. Advance care planning and the quality of end-of-life care in older adults. *Journal of the American Geriatrics Society* 61(2):209–214.

Bomba, P. 2005 (revised 2011). *Medical orders for life-sustaining treatment (MOLST): 8-step MOLST protocol.* https://molst.org/wp-content/uploads/2018/03/8StepProtocol.pdf (accessed December 17, 2020).

Bomba, P., and K. Orem. 2015. Lessons learned from New York's community approach to advance care planning and MOLST. *Annals of Palliative Medicine* 4(1):10–21.

Bond, W. F., M. Kim, C. M. Franciskovich, J. E. Weinberg, J. D. Svendsen, L. S. Fehr, A. Funk, R. Sawicki, and C. V. Asche. 2018. Advance care planning in an accountable care organization is associated with increased advanced directive documentation and decreased costs. *Journal of Palliative Medicine* 21(4):489–502.

Charles, C., and A. Gafni. 2006. Can I accurately predict the impact of an illness and its treatment on my future subjective well-being? A complex question that does not have a simple answer. *Health Expectations* 9(3):252–254.

Childers, J. W., D. B. White, and R. Arnold. 2021. "Has anything changed since then?": A framework to incorporate prior GOC conversations into decision making for acutely ill patients. *Journal of Pain and Symptom Management* 61(4):864–869.

Curtis, J. R., M. D. Wenrich, J. D. Carline, S. E. Shannon, D. M. Ambrozy, and P. G. Ramsey. 2001. Understanding physicians' skills at providing end-of-life care perspectives of patients, families, and health care workers. *Journal of General Internal Medicine* 16(1):41–49.

Detering, K. M., A. D. Hancock, M. C. Reade, and W. Silvester. 2010. The impact of advance care planning on end of life care in elderly patients: Randomised controlled trial. *BMJ* 340:c1345.

Elpern, E. H., B. Covert, and R. Kleinpell. 2005. Moral distress of staff nurses in a medical intensive care unit. *American Journal of Critical Care* 14(6):523–530.

Excellus BlueCross BlueShield. 2020. *Administrative data pull.* https://nysemolstregistry.com (restricted access).

Freytag, J., R. L. Street, Jr., D. E. Barnes, Y. Shi, A. M. Volow, J. K. Shim, S. C. Alexander, and R. L. Sudore. 2020. Empowering older adults to discuss advance care planning during clinical visits: The PREPARE randomized trial. *Journal of the American Geriatrics Society* 68(6):1210–1217.

Fried, T. R., E. H. Bradley, V. R. Towle, and H. Allore. 2002. Understanding the treatment preferences of seriously ill patients. *New England Journal of Medicine* 346(14):1061–1066.

Fried, T. R., A. L. Byers, W. T. Gallo, P. H. Van Ness, V. R. Towle, J. R. O'Leary, and J. A. Dubin. 2006. Prospective study of health status preferences and changes in preferences over time in older adults. *Archives of Internal Medicine* 166(8):890–895.

Gillick, M. R. 2004. Advance care planning. *New England Journal of Medicine* 350(1):7–8.

Guyatt, G., V. Montori, P. J. Devereaux, H. Schünemann, and M. Bhandari. 2004. Patients at the center: In our practice, and in our use of language. *ACP Journal Club* 140(1):A11–A12.

Halpern, J., and R. M. Arnold. 2008. Affective forecasting: An unrecognized challenge in making serious health decisions. *Journal of General Internal Medicine* 23(10):1708–1712.

Halpern, S. D. 2015. Toward evidence-based end-of-life care. *New England Journal of Medicine* 373(21):2001–2003.

Halpern, S. D., D. S. Small, A. B. Troxel, E. Cooney, B. Bayes, M. Chowdhury, H. E. Tomko, D. C. Angus, R. M. Arnold, G. Loewenstein, K. G. Volpp, D. B. White, and C. L. Bryce. 2020. Effect of default options in advance directives on hospital-free days and care choices among seriously ill patients: A randomized clinical trial. *JAMA Network Open* 3(3):e201742.

Heyland, D. K. 2020. Advance care planning (ACP) vs. advance serious illness preparations and planning (ASIPP). *Healthcare (Basel)* 8(3):218.

Heyland, D. K., C. Frank, D. Groll, D. Pichora, P. Dodek, G. Rocker, and A. Gafni. 2006. Understanding cardiopulmonary resuscitation decision making: Perspectives of seriously ill hospitalized patients and family members. *Chest* 130(2):419–428.

Heyland, D. K., P. Dodek, S. Mehta, D. Cook, A. Garland, H. T. Stelfox, S. M. Bagshaw, D. J. Kutsogiannis, K. Burns, J. Muscedere, A. F. Turgeon, R. Fowler, X. Jiang, and A. G. Day. 2015. Admission of the very elderly to the intensive care unit: Family members' perspectives on clinical decision-making from a multicenter cohort study. *Palliative Medicine* 29(4):324–335.

Heyland, D. K., R. Ilan, X. Jiang, J. J. You, and P. Dodek. 2016. The prevalence of medical error related to end-of-life communication in Canadian hospitals: Results of a multicentre observational study. *BMJ Quality and Safety* 25(9):671–679.

Heyland, D. K., R. Heyland, P. Dodek, J. J. You, T. Sinuff, T. Hiebert, X. Jiang, and A. G. Day. 2017. Discordance between patients' stated values and treatment preferences for end-of-life care: Results of a multicentre survey. *BMJ Supportive and Palliative Care* 7(3):292–299.

Heyland, D. K., R. Heyland, A. Bailey, and M. Howard. 2020. A novel decision aid to help plan for serious illness: A multisite randomized trial. *CMAJ Open* 8(2):E289–E296.

Hickman, S. E., C. A. Nelson, N. A. Perrin, A. H. Moss, B. J. Hammes, and S. W. Tolle. 2010. A comparison of methods to communicate treatment preferences in nursing facilities: Traditional practices versus the physician orders for life-sustaining treatment program. *Journal of the American Geriatrics Society* 58(7):1241–1248.

Houben, C. H. M., M. A. Spruit, M. T. J. Groenen, E. F. M. Wouters, and D. J. A. Janssen. 2014. Efficacy of advance care planning: A systematic review and meta-analysis. *Journal of the American Medical Directors Association* 15(7):477–489.

IOM (Institute of Medicine). 2015. *Dying in America: Improving quality and honoring individual preferences near the end of life.* Washington, DC: The National Academies Press.

Jadad, A. R., R. A. Moore, D. Carroll, C. Jenkinson, D. J. M. Reynolds, D. J. Gavaghan, and H. J. McQuay. 1996. Assessing the quality of reports of randomized clinical trials: Is blinding necessary? *Controlled Clinical Trials* 17(1):1–12.

Jimenez, G., W. S. Tan, A. K. Virk, C. K. Low, J. Car, and A. H. Y. Ho. 2018. Overview of systematic reviews of advance care planning: Summary of evidence and global lessons. *Journal of Pain and Symptom Management* 56(3):436–459.

Knight, T., A. Malyon, Z. Fritz, C. Subbe, T. Cooksley, M. Holland, and D. Lasserson. 2020. Advance care planning in patients referred to hospital for acute medical care: Results of a national day of care survey. *EClinicalMedicine* 19:100235.

Lakin, J. R., M. G. Robinson, Z. Obermeyer, B. W. Powers, S. D. Block, R. Cunningham, J. M. Tumblin, C. Vogeli, and R. E. Bernacki. 2019. Prioritizing primary care patients for a communication intervention using the "surprise question": A prospective cohort study. *Journal of General Internal Medicine* 34(8):1467–1474.

Lee, R. Y., L. C. Brumback, S. Sathitratanacheewin, W. B. Lober, M. E. Modes, Y. T. Lynch, C. I. Ambrose, J. Sibley, K. C. Vranas, D. R. Sullivan, R. A. Engelberg, J. R. Curtis, and E. K. Kross. 2020. Association of physician orders for life-sustaining treatment with ICU admission among patients hospitalized near the end of life. *JAMA* 323(10):950–960.

Lockhart, L. K., P. H. Ditto, J. H. Danks, K. M. Coppola, and W. D. Smucker. 2001. The stability of older adults' judgments of fates better and worse than death. *Death Studies* 25(4):299–317.

Loewenstein, G. 2005. Projection bias in medical decision making. *Medical Decision Making* 25(1):96–105.

Lyon, M. E., L. Squires, R. K. Scott, D. Benator, L. Briggs, I. Greenberg, L. J. D'Angelo, Y. I. Cheng, and J. Wang. 2020. Effect of family centered (FACE) advance care planning on longitudinal congruence in end-of-life treatment preferences: A randomized clinical trial. *AIDS and Behavior* 24(12):3359–3375.

Manz, C. R., R. B. Parikh, D. S. Small, C. N. Evans, C. Chivers, S. H. Regli, C. W. Hanson, J. E. Bekelman, C. A. L. Rareshide, N. O'Connor, L. M. Schuchter, L. N. Shulman, and M. S. Patel. 2020. Effect of integrating machine learning mortality estimates with behavioral nudges to clinicians on serious illness conversations among patients with cancer: A stepped-wedge cluster randomized clinical trial. *JAMA Oncology* 6(12):e204759.

Massachusetts Coalition for Serious Illness Care. 2019. *Advancing the language of advance care planning: A messaging research project*. http://maseriouscare.org/uploads/messaging-research-overview-updated-november-2019.pdf (accessed January 5, 2021).

McLeod, S. 2020. *Maslow's hierarchy of needs*. https://www.simplypsychology.org/maslow.html (accessed February 10, 2021).

McMahan, R. D., S. J. Knight, T. R. Fried, and R. L. Sudore. 2013. Advance care planning beyond advance directives: Perspectives from patients and surrogates. *Journal of Pain and Symptom Management* 46(3):355–365.

McMahan, R. D., I. Tellez, and R. L. Sudore. 2020. Deconstructing the complexities of advance care planning outcomes: What do we know and where do we go? A scoping review. *Journal of the American Geriatrics Society* 69(1):234–244.

Morrison, R. S. 2020. Advance directives/care planning: Clear, simple, and wrong. *Journal of Palliative Medicine* 23(7):878–879.

Pearlman, R. A., H. Starks, K. C. Cain, and W. G. Cole. 2005. Improvements in advance care planning in the Veterans Affairs system: Results of a multifaceted intervention. *Archives of Internal Medicine* 165(6):667–674.

Perkins, H. S. 2007. Controlling death: The false promise of advance directives. *Annals of Internal Medicine* 147(1):51–57.

Quill, T. E. 2000. Perspectives on care at the close of life. Initiating end-of-life discussions with seriously ill patients: Addressing the "elephant in the room." *JAMA* 284(19):2502–2507.

Rao, J. K., L. A. Anderson, F. C. Lin, and J. P. Laux. 2014. Completion of advance directives among U.S. consumers. *American Journal of Preventive Medicine* 46(1):65–70.

Rubin, E. B., A. E. Buehler, E. Cooney, N. B. Gabler, A. A. Mante, and S. D. Halpern. 2019. Intuitive vs. deliberative approaches to making decisions about life support: A randomized clinical trial. *JAMA Network Open* 2(1):e187851.

Sabatino, C. P. 2010. The evolution of health care advance planning law and policy. *The Milbank Quarterly* 88(2):211–239.

Scheunemann, L. P., N. C. Ernecoff, P. Buddadhumaruk, S. S. Carson, C. L. Hough, J. R. Curtis, W. G. Anderson, J. Steingrub, B. Lo, M. Matthay, R. M. Arnold, and D. B. White. 2019. Clinician-family communication about patients' values and preferences in intensive care units. *JAMA Internal Medicine* 179(5):676–684.

Sessanna, L., and M. A. Jezewski. 2008. Advance directive decision making among independent community-dwelling older adults: A systematic review of health science literature. *Journal of Applied Gerontology* 27(4):486–510.

Sharp, T., E. Moran, I. Kuhn, and S. Barclay. 2013. Do the elderly have a voice? Advance care planning discussions with frail and older individuals: A systematic literature review and narrative synthesis. *British Journal of General Practice* 63(615):e657–e668.

Silveira, M. J., S. Y. Kim, and K. M. Langa. 2010. Advance directives and outcomes of surrogate decision making before death. *New England Journal of Medicine* 362(13):1211–1218.

Singer, P. A., D. K. Martin, and M. Kelner. 1999. Quality end-of-life care: Patients' perspectives. *JAMA* 281(2):163–168.

Sinuff, T., P. Dodek, J. J. You, D. Barwick, C. Tayler, J. Downar, M. Hartwick, C. Frank, H. T. Stelfox, and D. K. Heyland. 2015. Improving end-of-life communication and decision making: The development of a conceptual framework and quality indicators. *Journal of Pain and Symptom Management* 49(6):1070–1080.

Steinhauser, K. E., E. C. Clipp, M. McNeilly, N. A. Christakis, L. M. McIntyre, and J. A. Tulsky. 2000. In search of a good death: Observations of patients, families, and providers. *Annals of Internal Medicine* 132(10):825–832.

Sudore, R. L., and T. R. Fried. 2010. Redefining the "planning" in advance care planning: Preparing for end-of-life decision making. *Annals of Internal Medicine* 153(4):256–261.

Sudore, R. L., H. D. Lum, J. J. You, L. C. Hanson, D. E. Meier, S. Z. Pantilat, D. D. Matlock, J. A. C. Rietjens, I. J. Korfage, C. S. Ritchie, J. S. Kutner, J. M. Teno, J. Thomas, R. D. McMahan, and D. K. Heyland. 2017. Defining advance care planning for adults: A consensus definition from a multidisciplinary Delphi panel. *Journal of Pain and Symptom Management* 53(5):821–832.

Sudore, R. L., D. K. Heyland, H. D. Lum, J. A. C. Rietjens, I. J. Korfage, C. S. Ritchie, L. C. Hanson, D. E. Meier, S. Z. Pantilat, K. Lorenz, M. Howard, M. J. Green, J. E. Simon, M. A. Feuz, and J. J. You. 2018a. Outcomes that define successful advance care planning: A Delphi panel consensus. *Journal of Pain and Symptom Management* 55(2):245–255.

Sudore, R. L., D. Schillinger, M. T. Katen, Y. Shi, W. J. Boscardin, S. Osua, and D. E. Barnes. 2018b. Engaging diverse English- and Spanish-speaking older adults in advance care planning: The PREPARE randomized clinical trial. *JAMA Internal Medicine* 178(12):1616–1625.

Sudore, R. L., D. Schillinger, A. Volow, Y. Shi, J. Boscardin, J. Shim, M. T. Katen, S. J. Osua, R. A. Ramos, B. Li, A. Herrera, B. Quintanilla, R. McMahan, M. Fuez, C. Juarez, F. Quintanilla, and D. E. Barnes. 2020. *Preparing Spanish-speaking older adults for advance care planning and medical decision-making—the PREPARE trial.* Washington, DC: Patient-Centered Outcomes Research Institute.

The Economist. 2016. The right to die: What is unbearable? https://www.economist.com/science-and-technology/2016/08/04/what-is-unbearable (accessed February 16, 2021).

Torke, A. M., M. Siegler, A. Abalos, R. M. Moloney, and G. C. Alexander. 2009. Physicians' experience with surrogate decision making for hospitalized adults. *Journal of General Internal Medicine* 24(9):1023–1028.

Ubel, P. A. 2005. Emotions, decisions, and the limits of rationality: Symposium introduction. *Medical Decision Making* 25(1):95–96.

Ubel, P. A., G. Loewenstein, N. Schwarz, and D. Smith. 2005. Misimagining the unimaginable: The disability paradox and health care decision making. *Health Psychology* 24(4S):S57–S62.

Ulrich, C. M., and C. Grady. 2019. *Moral distress and moral strength among clinicians in health care systems: A call for research.* NAM Perspectives. Commentary, National Academy of Medicine, Washington, DC. https://doi.org/10.31478/201909c.

U.S. Supreme Court. 1990. *Cruzan v. Director, Missouri Department of Health. West's Supreme Court Reporter* 110:2841–2892.

Waller, A., R. Sanson-Fisher, B. R. Nair, and T. Evans. 2019. Are older and seriously ill inpatients planning ahead for future medical care? *BMC Geriatrics* 19(1):212.

Wenrich, M. D., J. R. Curtis, S. E. Shannon, J. D. Carline, D. M. Ambrozy, and P. G. Ramsey. 2001. Communicating with dying patients within the spectrum of medical care from terminal diagnosis to death. *Archives of Internal Medicine* 161(6):868–874.

Winter, L., M. P. Lawton, and K. Ruckdeschel. 2003. Preferences for prolonging life: A prospect theory approach. *International Journal of Aging and Human Development* 56(2):155–170.

Yadav, K. N., N. B. Gabler, E. Cooney, S. Kent, J. Kim, N. Herbst, A. Mante, S. D. Halpern, and K. R. Courtright. 2017. Approximately one in three U.S. adults completes any type of advance directive for end-of-life care. *Health Affairs* 36(7):1244–1251.

You, J. J., J. Downar, R. A. Fowler, F. Lamontagne, I. W. Ma, D. Jayaraman, J. Kryworuchko, P. H. Strachan, R. Ilan, A. P. Nijjar, J. Neary, J. Shik, K. Brazil, A. Patel, K. Wiebe, M. Albert, A. Palepu, E. Nouvet, A. R. des Ordons, N. Sharma, A. Abdul-Razzak, X. Jiang, A. Day, and D. K. Heyland. 2015. Barriers to goals of care discussions with seriously ill hospitalized patients and their families: A multicenter survey of clinicians. *JAMA Internal Medicine* 175(4):549–556.

# Appendix A

# Statement of Task

An ad hoc planning committee of the National Academies of Sciences, Engineering, and Medicine will organize and host a 1-day public workshop that will explore the current state of advance care planning (ACP) and examine the role of effective communication across the lifespan about the care and treatment preferences of patients facing serious illness. The workshop will feature invited presentations and panel discussions on topics that may include ways to

- Improve communication between clinicians and patients and their families,
- Coordinate ACP discussions across care transitions,
- Achieve and measure goal-concordant care,
- Assess the impact of effective ACP on patient outcomes and health care spending,
- Incorporate ACP in electronic health records,
- Overcome challenges with health literacy and cultural competency, and
- Educate and involve younger generations in ACP.

The planning committee will develop the agenda for the workshop, select and invite speakers and discussants, and moderate the discussions. A proceedings of the presentations and discussions at the workshop will be prepared by a designated rapporteur in accordance with institutional guidelines.

# Appendix B

# Workshop Agenda

**WEBINAR 1: OCTOBER 26, 2020**
**12:00 PM – 2:30 PM ET**

12:00 PM  Welcome from the Roundtable on Quality Care for People with Serious Illness

**Peggy Maguire, J.D.**
Cambia Health Foundation

**James Tulsky, M.D.**
Harvard Medical School, Brigham and Women's Hospital, and Dana-Farber Cancer Institute

*Roundtable Co-Chairs*

12:05 PM  Overview of the Webinar Series

**Robert Arnold, M.D.**
Distinguished Service Professor of Medicine, Chief, Section of Palliative Care and Medical Ethics
Director, Institute for Doctor–Patient Communication
Medical Director, University of Pittsburgh Medical Center Palliative and Supportive Institute
University of Pittsburgh Department of Medicine

**JoAnne Reifsnyder, Ph.D., M.B.A., M.S.N., FAAN**
Executive Vice President, Clinical Operations
Chief Nursing Officer, Genesis HealthCare
*Representing the Hospice and Palliative Nurses Association*

*Planning Committee Co-Chairs*

**12:10 PM**    **Session One: The Paradox of Advance Care Planning**

*Moderator:*

**JoAnne Reifsnyder, Ph.D., M.B.A., M.S.N., FAAN**
Genesis HealthCare

*Speakers:*

**Maurine Stuart**
Volunteer, National Patient Advocate Foundation

**Wyvonia Woods Harris**
Volunteer, National Patient Advocate Foundation

**Bernard Lo, M.D.**
President Emeritus, The Greenwall Foundation

**Rebecca Sudore, M.D.**
Professor, University of California, San Francisco, School of Medicine

**12:50 PM**    **Audience Q&A**

**1:10 PM**    **Session Two: Interpreting the Evidence Base for Advance Care Planning**

*Moderator:*

**Susan E. Hickman, Ph.D.**
Director, Indiana University Center for Aging Research, Regenstrief Institute
Professor, Indiana University Schools of Nursing and Medicine
Cornelius and Yvonne Pettinga Chair in Aging Research
Codirector, IUPUI RESPECT Signature Center

APPENDIX B                                                            *73*

>   *Speakers:*
>
>   **Sean Morrison, M.D.**
>   Ellen and Howard C. Katz Professor and Chair, Brookdale
>      Department of Geriatrics and Palliative Medicine
>   Director, National Palliative Care Research Center
>   Icahn School of Medicine at Mount Sinai
>
>   **Carole Montgomery, M.D., FHM, M.H.S.A.**
>   Executive Medical Director, Respecting Choices
>
>   **Daren Heyland, M.D., M.Sc., FRCPC**
>   Professor, Internal Medicine, Critical Care
>   Queen's University School of Medicine
>
>   **Patricia Bomba, M.D., MACP, FRCP**
>   Vice President and Medical Director, Geriatrics
>   Excellus BlueCross BlueShield

1:50 PM   **Panel Discussion**

2:10 PM   **Audience Q&A**

2:25 PM   **Closing Remarks**

2:30 PM   **Webinar Adjourns**

## WEBINAR 2: NOVEMBER 2, 2020
## 12:00 PM – 2:30 PM ET

12:00 PM   **Welcome from the Roundtable on Quality Care for People with Serious Illness**

>   **Peggy Maguire, J.D.**
>   Cambia Health Foundation
>
>   **James Tulsky, M.D.**
>   Harvard Medical School, Brigham and Women's Hospital,
>      and Dana-Farber Cancer Institute
>
>   *Roundtable Co-Chairs*

**12:05 PM**  Overview of the Webinar Series

**Robert Arnold, M.D.**
Distinguished Service Professor of Medicine, Chief, Section of Palliative Care and Medical Ethics
Director, Institute for Doctor–Patient Communication
Medical Director, University of Pittsburgh Medical Center Palliative and Supportive Institute
University of Pittsburgh Department of Medicine

**JoAnne Reifsnyder, Ph.D., M.B.A., M.S.N., FAAN**
Executive Vice President, Clinical Operations
Chief Nursing Officer, Genesis HealthCare
*Representing the Hospice and Palliative Nurses Association*

*Planning Committee Co-Chairs*

**12:10 PM**  Brief Summary of the First Webinar

**Susan E. Hickman, Ph.D.**
Director, Indiana University Center for Aging Research, Regenstrief Institute
Professor, Indiana University Schools of Nursing and Medicine
Cornelius and Yvonne Pettinga Chair in Aging Research
Codirector, IUPUI RESPECT Signature Center

**12:15 PM**  Session Three: Thinking Differently About Advance Care Planning

*Moderator:*

**Kimberly Johnson, M.D.**
Associate Professor of Medicine
Duke University School of Medicine

*Speakers:*

**Scott Halpern, M.D., Ph.D.**
John M. Eisenberg Professor of Medicine, Epidemiology, and Medical Ethics and Health Policy
Director, Palliative and Advanced Illness Research Center
University of Pennsylvania Perelman School of Medicine

**Rebecca Dresser, J.D.**
Daniel Noyes Kirby Professor of Law Emerita
Washington University

**Anna Gosline, M.P.H.**
Senior Director of Strategic Initiatives, Blue Cross Blue Shield of Massachusetts
Executive Director, Massachusetts Coalition for Serious Illness Care

**12:50 PM**    **Audience Q&A**

**1:05 PM**    **Session Four: Practical Steps to More Effective Advance Care Planning**

*Moderator:*

**Hillary Lum, M.D.**
Associate Professor, Medicine—Geriatrics
University of Colorado School of Medicine

*Speakers:*

**Rebecca Kirch, J.D.**
Executive Vice President, Policy and Programs
National Patient Advocate Foundation

**Julie Childers, M.D.**
Associate Professor of Medicine, Division of General Internal Medicine, University of Pittsburgh

**Nina Ross O'Connor, M.D.**
Chief of Palliative Care, Penn Medicine

**1:40 PM**    **Audience Q&A**

**1:55 PM**    **Panel Discussion**

*Moderator:*

**Robert Arnold, M.D.**
University of Pittsburgh Department of Medicine

*Panelists:*

**Diane Meier, M.D., FACP**
Director, Center to Advance Palliative Care

**Reverend Cynthia Carter Perrilliat, M.P.A.**
Executive Director, Alameda County Care Alliance

**Millie Solomon, Ph.D.**
President, The Hastings Center

**Ab Brody, Ph.D., R.N., FAAN**
Associate Professor of Nursing and Medicine
Associate Director, Hartford Institute for Geriatric Nursing
New York University Rory Meyers College of Nursing

**2:25 PM**     **Closing Remarks/Wrap-Up for the Webinar Series**

**2:30 PM**     **Webinar Adjourns**